# THE CALIFORNIA DIRECTORY OF
# FINE WINERIES

SECOND EDITION

# THE CALIFORNIA DIRECTORY OF
# FINE WINERIES

K. REKA BADGER AND CHERYL CRABTREE, WRITERS

ROBERT HOLMES, PHOTOGRAPHER

TOM SILBERKLEIT, EDITOR AND PUBLISHER

WINE HOUSE PRESS

# CONTENTS

# INTRODUCTION

Navigating California's burgeoning Central Coast wine country can be intimidating. Hundreds of wineries—from enchanting estates to storefront tasting rooms, from nationally recognized labels to hidden gems—can be found throughout the counties of Santa Barbara and San Luis Obispo. They are waiting to be discovered. The challenge is in deciding where to go and how to plan a trip. This book will be your indispensable traveling companion.

The fifty-one wineries in this fully updated, second edition of *The California Directory of Fine Wineries, Central Coast*, are known for producing some of the region's most admired wines. From the moment you walk into these wineries and tasting rooms, you will be invited to converse and sample at a leisurely tempo. In this down-to-earth wine country, passionate vineyard owners and winemakers enjoy experimenting and strive to make distinctive wines that please themselves as well as their devoted customers. Whether you are a novice wine taster or a longtime connoisseur, I suggest that you try unfamiliar wines. You'll be rewarded with outstanding blends and local specialties often unavailable elsewhere.

Although the quality of the winemaker's art is of paramount importance, the wineries are also notable as tourist destinations. Many feature distinctive contemporary architecture. Others are housed in meticulously preserved historic structures. Some host food-and-wine pairings, barrel tastings, art exhibits, concerts, grape stomps, and weekend barbecues. You will also enjoy taking informative behind-the-scenes tours, strolling through colorful gardens, and picnicking on the edge of the vineyards.

As you explore this region, you'll encounter some of California's most appealing scenery and attractions—mountain ranges, dramatic coastline, abundant parkland, and historic towns. Use the information in this book to plan your trip, and be sure to stop along the way to take in the sights. You have my promise that traveling to your destination will be as pleasurable as the wine tasted upon your welcome.

— Tom Silberkleit
Editor and Publisher
Wine House Press
Sonoma, California

# What Is an Appellation?

Winemakers often showcase the source of their fruit by citing an *appellation,* a word that refers to the geographical area where the wine grapes were grown. An appellation is a specific growing region that, in the United States, is usually determined by borders such as state and county lines, rather than by geography. When an appellation, such as Edna Valley or Santa Maria Valley, appears on a wine label, it indicates that at least 85 percent of the fruit for the wine came from that area.

Although frequently used interchangeably, the terms "appellation of origin" and "American Viticultural Area" (AVA) are not synonymous. AVAs, in contrast to appellations, are defined by natural features: soil types, climate, and topography such as rivers and mountain ranges. The U.S. Alcohol and Tobacco Tax and Trade Bureau (TTB) defines the characteristics of an AVA and has the authority to approve or deny applications for new AVAs. When wineries or other interested parties want to create an AVA, they must submit documented research to the TTB proving that the area has enough specific attributes to clearly distinguish it from surrounding areas.

Winemakers know that identifying the origin of the grapes can lend prestige to a wine, particularly if the appellation has earned a reputation for high quality. Naming a wine's source also provides valuable information about what's inside the bottle. For instance, a Pinot Noir from the hundred-square-mile Santa Rita Hills appellation (abbreviated Sta. Rita Hills to distinguish it from a similarly named appellation in Chile) is likely to vary significantly from one sourced from the more generic California appellation, which includes grapes from all over the state. Moreover, informed consumers and wine connoisseurs know that a Chardonnay from the Santa Maria Valley, for example, is apt to display different aromas and flavors than a Chardonnay originating in Paso Robles.

When a winery located in one appellation uses grapes from another appellation to make a particular wine, the label indicates the source of the fruit, rather than the physical location of the winery. For instance, Thacher Winery, in the Paso Robles appellation, sometimes sources Syrah from Monterey County. Hence the label reads "Thacher Winery Syrah, Coast View Vineyard, Monterey County."

Santa Barbara and San Luis Obispo counties currently contain or are located within the following appellations:

| Santa Barbara County | San Luis Obispo County |
| --- | --- |
| Central Coast | Arroyo Grande Valley |
| Happy Canyon of Santa Barbara | Central Coast |
| Santa Maria Bench (proposed viticultural area) | Edna Valley |
| Santa Maria Valley | Paso Robles |
| Santa Ynez Valley | Santa Maria Valley |
| Sta. Rita Hills | York Mountain |

# THE MAKING OF WINE

Most vintners agree that wine is made not in the cellar, but in the vineyard, where sun, soil, and water—collectively known as *terroir*—impart varietal flavor. Growers select vineyard sites for many reasons, including exposure and low fertility, because lean soils often produce the most flavorful fruit. Based on the *terroir,* they plant varietals and clones (also called subvarietals) that will grow best, and then wait three years or longer for the vines to mature before ever picking a grape.

Harvest brings intense activity, as truckloads of ripe grapes roll into the winery, ready to be crushed and destemmed. After crush, white grapes are pressed, and their juice sent to barrels or stainless steel tanks for fermentation, while red grapes are fermented with skins and all to provide additional color and flavor. Winemakers introduce commercially grown yeast or sometimes rely on ambient wild yeast to trigger fermentation, a roiling process during which yeast converts grape sugar into alcohol and carbon dioxide. Fermentation stops when the yeast runs out of sugar, which results in a dry wine. Conversely, the winemaker may quickly chill the wine, killing the yeast and leaving behind a little residual sugar for sweetness.

After fermentation, many wines spend from a few months to a year or more in oak barrels where they develop complexity and absorb hints of the toasted interior of the barrel itself. Red wines usually rest in the barrel longer than whites. Most rosés and crisp white wines, such as Riesling, spend little or no time in the barrel.

Throughout the process, winemakers taste their young wares, checking for signs of spoilage and imbalance. They analyze samples in a laboratory to determine the chemical makeup of the wine, which helps them to correct potential problems and maintain stability as the wines continue to evolve. Prior to bottling, vintners spend hours tasting wine from tanks and barrels to come up with optimum combinations for their final blends. Once in the bottle, rosés and light, fruity whites are usually released within a few months. Robust reds remain at the winery for several months to a year or so, which gives them a chance to mature and soften before their release.

To make sparkling wine using the *méthode champenoise,* vintners combine a blended base wine—usually Chardonnay or Pinot Noir fermented without the skins—with sugar and yeast. The mixture goes into heavy glass bottles, where a secondary fermentation takes place, giving the wine its signature bubbles. The wine ages for a year or more, and then dead yeast cells are removed in a process called disgorging, a little wine is added back to the bottle, and a natural cork is wired in place.

Wine lovers often buy several bottles of a favorite vintage and store them in a cellar or cool closet. That way, they can open a bottle every year or so, and enjoy the subtle flavor shifts as the wine continues to mature over time.

# THE ART OF BARREL MAKING

Since ancient times, skilled artisans, called coopers, have made an array of casks for many purposes, including storage and shipping. Dry casks, often crafted of pine and cedar, held tobacco, flour, and other dry goods. A barrel is a cask designed to hold liquids, including wine. Handmade barrels reflect the highest form of the art of cooperage.

Until recent decades, French oak prevailed as the best type of wood for wine storage. During the Napoleonic era, the French planted a number of oak forests to supply the shipbuilding industry. Each forest produced trees with divergent character traits, and barrels made of wood from certain forests had distinct effects on the wine stored within them. In the early years of the U.S. wine industry, American oak seemed to overpower wine flavor. However, research determined that the strong influence came from the way people were preparing the wood and building the barrels. Today many wineries use American oak barrels, which are typically more affordable than their French counterparts. Some wineries also seek out Hungarian oak barrels, which yield distinctive flavors at a lower price point than French and American.

Barrel making begins with experts choosing high-quality wood by looking at tree shapes, growing conditions, and wood grain, as well as the presence of tannins, compounds that influence the flavor of wine. The best wood usually comes from older trees, more than a hundred years of age and at least five feet in diameter. Ideal wood should be straight and have no knots or burrs, and only traces of sap and regular rings. Workers split the logs into staves by hand, to avoid damage to veins in the wood grain, which could cause leakage in barrels. Then they plane the staves and store them outdoors in tiers for about three years to age naturally in wet and dry weather. This allows the wood to mellow out elements that could overpower the wine, such as tannins, scents, and impurities. Winemakers often choose barrels made of tough, porous white oak, which usually matures well in these conditions. When the staves are ready, they are cut and prepared for the cooper.

Barrels take about eight hours to complete. The cooper begins by "raising the barrel"—he takes premium staves and places them in a jig, a metal hoop that holds the staves fast. He pushes three hoops into place and waters the staves, then "toasts" them on a fire to the desired type to suit the wine grape and style: typically light, medium, or heavy. Lightly toasted barrels impart more oak flavor, while heavily toasted barrels give wines a charred or "roasted" aroma and smoky, spicy notes. The heat and moisture make the staves flexible enough for the cooper to take a winch and bend the staves into a barrel shape, tie them with trusses, and place the remaining iron or metal hoops around them. He carves a croze, or groove, in the ends to hold the flat, round barrel ends. Then he seals the ends with a dowel and river reed and finishes the barrel with mallet, plane, and sandpaper.

Barrels are heavy—they weigh up to 140 pounds when empty and much more when filled with wine. But the cylindrical shape allows workers to roll and turn barrels for easy transport. Winemakers use each barrel for about five to seven years. At that point, the porous wood fibers have absorbed as much wine as they can tolerate. They also have little flavor left to convey to the wine stored within. Thereafter, many barrels continue to contribute to winery life as planters, furniture, and wine-themed artistic creations.

# MODERN STOPPERS:
## CORK, PLASTIC, AND SCREWCAPS

It's an ancient question: What is the best way to close a wine bottle? Since the late 1600s, vintners have largely chosen stoppers made from cork tree bark. These time-tested closures usually provide an effective seal, potentially lasting as long as thirty years or more. At the same time, they are elastic and compressible, which allows for easy extraction. Many wine aficionados associate cork stoppers with a hallowed ritual, using corkscrews or other devices to remove the cork and launch the wine appreciation experience.

Corks, however, are not perfect stoppers. In past years, statistics estimated that nearly 20 percent of wine bottles were damaged by cork problems, chiefly from "cork taint." This results from natural airborne fungi meeting up with unnatural chemical compounds (pollut-ants from industrial sources, for example, pesticides and wood preservatives). The compounds contaminate the cork bark and produce other chemicals that give the wine a musty odor. Contaminated corks occasion-ally disintegrate and crumble in the bottle. Some corks fail by allowing too much oxygen to pass through to the wine. Cork advocates claim that recent research has reduced the risk of cork taint to as little as 1 percent. Any risk at all is unac-ceptable to some winemakers, who now rely on other types of bottle stoppers.

Screwcaps, once associated with inexpensive, mass-produced wines, have grown increasingly popular in many countries around the world. The caps hold in place a seal liner, designed to allow a microscopic amount of breathabil-ity for aging wines over time. Screwcaps are easy to remove—all you need is an opposable thumb—and screwcap advocates say that even a monkey can open a bottle. More and more wineries are using screwcaps with great success, virtually eliminating the occurrence of damaged wine due to closure problems.

Synthetic (plastic) stoppers also offer a reliable sealing solution. They act in the same manner as corks and are removed from bottles with corkscrews, pulls, and other devices. Synthetic corks can provide an excellent seal. However, they are not as flexible as cork, and a highly effective seal makes them difficult to remove from the bottle. They are thus designed to oxidize and lose their elasticity within a few years and are not good candidates for long-term storage in wine cellars. These stoppers are best used for wines consumed upon release or soon thereafter.

Choice of stoppers also involves environmental considerations. The western Mediterranean region contains 6.6 million acres of cork oak tree (*Quercus suber*) forests. Bark from mature trees is harvested in environmentally friendly fashion every nine years, and trees typically live from 150 to 200 years. Cork stoppers are natural, renewable, recyclable, and biodegradable. The forests support wildlife habitats, absorb carbon dioxide from the atmosphere, and sustain local workers. Plastic can be recycled, but it is not made from environmentally friendly material and is not a sustainable product. Screwcaps are recyclable, but the manufacturing process requires much energy usage and releases greenhouses gases into the atmosphere.

As the stopper debate continues to rock the wine world, some wineries are returning to a simple, environmentally friendly solution used for centuries. They sell whole barrels directly to restaurants and tasting rooms, which offer "barrel wines" on tap to customers—no stoppers, bottles, or packaging at all.

# THE FOOD AND WINE CONNECTION

The Central Coast boasts cultural and lifestyle advantages associated with urban centers, yet remains at heart an agricultural region. In Santa Barbara and San Luis Obispo counties, more than 50 percent of the combined acreage supports livestock and food crops. Local farmers supply markets and restaurants with such Central Coast specialties as avocados, strawberries, heritage apples, and heirloom tomatoes. Ranchers provide fresh eggs, sausage, and grass-fed beef, lamb, pork, buffalo, venison, and chicken. Along the coast, shellfish wranglers tend briny beds of abalone and oysters, and hard-working fishermen bring in fresh seafood daily. Area purveyors supplement the bounty with crusty breads and baked goods, extra-virgin olive oils, and artisanal cheeses.

Most of the region's edible delights can be found at farmers' markets taking place every day somewhere on the Central Coast. One of the largest in California is held every Thursday night in downtown San Luis Obispo. Part open-air market, part street fair, it features more than 120 vendors tending tables brimming with seasonal produce, meats, honey, nuts, and cut flowers. Grill masters dish up sizzling sausage, ribs, and tri-tip sandwiches from aromatic barbecues, and musical groups play on just about every side street. Jugglers, unicyclists, puppeteers, and dancers lend a festive flavor to the popular market.

The Central Coast's agricultural wealth, along with its dynamic culture, attracts world-class chefs and drives culinary innovation. Encouraged by supportive communities, these chefs riff on the cuisines of Asia, Latin America, Europe, and the Mediterranean countries. They dish up distinctly local fare, too, including Santa Maria–style barbecue, based on the mid-nineteenth-century feasts served by cattlemen during roundups and fiestas. The centerpiece of the meal is grilled beef: either top-block or tri-tip, a triangular cut of sirloin traditionally ground into hamburger. It is served with salsa, small savory pink beans called *pinquitos,* green salad, and garlic bread. In the mid-1950s, a Santa Maria–area butcher grilled a tri-tip as an experiment, gave away juicy slices to customers, and ignited a food trend. Today, the beef is rubbed with a mixture of garlic, salt, and pepper and cooked slowly over a glowing red oak fire.

Naturally, contemporary chefs often pair their creations with local wines. Winemaking began on the Central Coast in 1782 when Franciscan missionaries planted grapevines near the city of Santa Barbara. By the turn of the twenty-first century, Santa Barbara and San Luis Obispo counties were home to more than 50,000 vineyard acres supporting fifty-five different varieties of wine grapes. The counties' three-hundred-plus wineries produce an astonishing array of wines, including Rhône-, Burgundy-, and Bordeaux-style offerings, Cal-Italian blends, and distinctly regional wines.

Home to bustling cities and two renowned universities, the Central Coast offers the benefits of urban life in a wonderfully pastoral environment. With their fertile fields, magnificent coastline, and thriving vinicultural scene, Santa Barbara and San Luis Obispo counties provide all the elements for a perfect connection of food and wine.

# READING A WINE LABEL

When you encounter an unfamiliar bottle of wine, you can learn a lot about it from inspecting the label. Federal law requires wineries to print specific information on the front label of each bottle. Some wineries include details on how a wine was made or how well it will pair with specific foods, usually on a separate label on the back of the bottle.

Most prominently displayed on the label is the name of the winery or the brand name. Also given emphasis is the type of wine. In most cases, this is the grape varietal, such as Chardonnay or Zinfandel. To carry the name of a varietal, the wine must be made of 75 percent of that varietal. Wineries can also use a generic name or a proprietary one such as Tablas Creek Vineyard's Esprit de Beaucastel.

The place of origin on the label tells you where the grapes were grown, not necessarily where the wine was made. A label bearing the name "California" means that 100 percent of the grapes were grown within the state. To use a county name, 75 percent of the grapes must come from that county. To use an American Viticultural Area (AVA) or appellation, at least 85 percent of the grapes must come from the defined area. The vintage is the year the grapes were harvested, not the year the wine was released. The wine must contain at least 95 percent of the stated vintage. Labels sometimes identify an individual vineyard. This is a way for the winemaker to indicate that the grapes came from an exceptional source. To be a vineyard-designated wine, a minimum of 95 percent of the grapes must have come from the vineyard named. Any wine with an alcohol content of more than 14 percent must carry this information. Wines designated as "table wine," with 7 to 14 percent alcohol content, are not required to state such information. American-made wine that contains sulfites must say so on the front or back label. Sulfur dioxide is a natural by-product of winemaking. Some wineries also add sulfites as a preservative.

Other information found on labels may include the description "estate bottled." This tells you that the winery owns (or controls) the vineyard where the grapes were grown and that both the winery and the vineyard are in the same AVA. A bottle labeled "reserve" indicates that the wine is of a superior quality compared with the winery's nonreserve offerings.

Labels for sparkling wines may contain the term *méthode champenoise*. The most salient feature of this process is allowing the wine to ferment for a second time inside the bottle, resulting in bubbles that are finer than those in sparkling wine made by other methods. Vintage sparkling wines are designated as either regular vintage or *prestige cuvée* (also called *tête de cuvée* or premium vintage), meaning that the wine is the top of the line.

# THE ETIQUETTE OF WINE TASTING

Most of the wineries profiled in this book offer amenities ranging from inviting gardens to winemaker dinners, but their main attraction is the tasting room. This is where winery employees get a chance to share their products and knowledge with consumers, in hopes of establishing a lifelong relationship. They are there to please.

Yet, for some visitors, the ritual of tasting fine wines can be intimidating. Perhaps it's because swirling wine and using a spit bucket seem to be unnatural acts. But with a few tips, even a first-time taster can enjoy the experience.

After all, the point of tasting is to enhance your knowledge by learning the differences among varieties of wines, styles of winemaking, and appellations. A list of available wines is usually posted, beginning with whites and ending with the heaviest reds or, if available, dessert wines. Look for the tasting notes, which are typically set out on the counter; refer to them as you taste each wine.

After you are served, hold the stem of the glass with your thumb and as many fingers as you need to maintain control. Lift the glass up to the light and note the color and intensity of the wine. Good wines tend to be bright, with the color fading near the rim. Next, gently swirl the wine in the glass. Observe how much of the wine adheres to the sides of the glass. If lines—called legs—are visible, the wine is viscous, indicating body or weight as well as a high alcohol content. Now, tip the glass to about a 45-degree angle, take a short sniff, and concentrate on the aromas. Swirl the wine again to aerate it, releasing additional aromas. Take another sniff and see if the "bouquet" reminds you of anything —rose petals, citrus fruit, or a freshly ironed pillowcase, for example—that will help you identify the aroma.

Finally, take a sip and swirl the wine around your tongue, letting your taste buds pick up all the flavors. The wine may remind you of honey or cherries or mint—as with the "nosing," try to make as many associations as you can. Then spit the wine into the bucket on the counter. Afterward, notice how long the flavor stays in your mouth; a long finish is the ideal. If you don't want another taste, just pour the wine remaining in your glass into the bucket and move on. Remember, the more you spit or pour out, the more wines you can sample.

The next level of wine tasting involves guided tastings and food-and-wine pairings. In these sessions, a few cheeses or appetizers are paired with a flight of wines, usually a selection of three red or three white wines presented in the recommended order of tasting. The server will explain what goes with what.

If you still feel self-conscious, practice at home. Once you are in a real tasting room, you'll be better able to focus on the wine itself. That's the real payoff, because once you learn what you like and why you like it, you'll be able to recognize wines in a similar vein anywhere in the world.

SANTA
BARBARA
COUNTY

One of the world's extraordinary geographic anomalies defines Santa Barbara County wine country. Rather than being oriented north-south, the mountain ranges run east-west. The towering peaks and sloping hillsides funnel cool winds and fog from the Pacific Ocean through river valleys, resulting in an incredible geographic diversity and a superior environment for growing premium wine grapes.

Until the late 1960s, only a handful of vineyards existed here. After University of California scientific research pointed to the area's potential as a premier wine-grape region, pioneering vintners planted vines with little other than instinct to guide them. Their experiences and successes—especially with award-winning Pinot Noir and Chardonnay—helped put Santa Barbara County on the international wine map. Today the county boasts more than 23,000 acres of vineyards. Of the county's many wineries, more than half produce fewer than 2,000 cases a year.

Vineyards, interspersed with organic farms, thoroughbred horse ranches, and cattle ranches, blanket the rural landscape north of the Santa Ynez Mountains. Two-lane roads connect the small Danish-themed town of Solvang with the Old West villages of Los Olivos and Santa Ynez, and picturesque Highway 246 winds westward through Buellton and the Santa Rita Hills to the westernmost city of Lompoc. These uncrowded roads attract cycling enthusiasts from around the world, who enjoy pedaling for miles in a stunning pastoral setting. They also come to train and compete in major international races such as the annual Tour of California. The vast Los Padres National Forest bounds the eastern sectors. On the south side, the wild beaches of the rugged Gaviota coast stretch forty miles to the vibrant city of Santa Barbara.

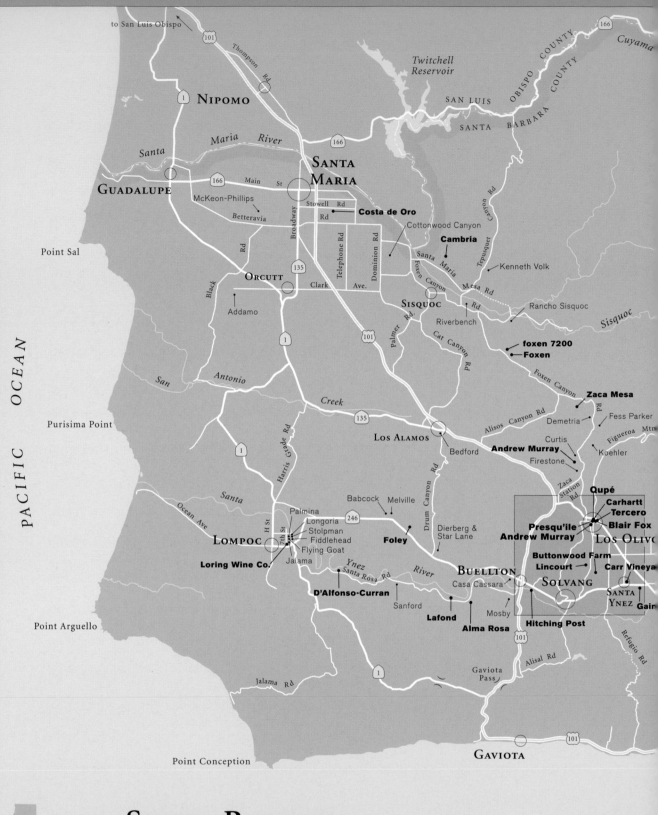

to San Luis Obispo

101

Thompson Rd

1  **NIPOMO**

*Santa    Maria    River*

*Santa*

**GUADALUPE**

166    Main    St

McKeon-Phillips

Betteravia

Point Sal

Black    Rd

**ORCUTT**

135

Addamo

Clark    Ave.

Telephone Rd

Broadway

Dominion Rd

Stowell    Rd

Rd

**Costa de Oro**

Cottonwood Canyon

**Cambria**

*Santa Maria*

Foxen Canyon

Mesa Rd

Rd

Kenneth Volk

Rancho Sisquoc

**SISQUOC**

Riverbench

*Sisquoc*

Palmer Rd

Cat Canyon Rd

**foxen 7200**
**Foxen**

*Twitchell Reservoir*

166

**SANTA MARIA**

SAN LUIS OBISPO COUNTY

SANTA    BARBARA    COUNTY

*Cuyama*

166

Tepusquet Canyon Rd

Foxen Canyon

**Zaca Mesa**

Rd    Fess Parker

PACIFIC    OCEAN

Purisima Point

1

San    Antonio    Creek

135

1

Harris Grade Rd

**LOS ALAMOS**

Bedford

Drum Canyon Rd

Alisos Canyon Rd

Demetria

Curtis

**Andrew Murray**

Firestone

Figueroa Mtn

Koehler

Zaca Station Rd

**Qupé**
**Carhartt**
**Tercero**

**Presqu'ile**    **Blair Fox**
**Andrew Murray**    **LOS OLIVO**

*Santa*

Ocean Ave

H St

7th St

**Palmina**
**Longoria**
**Stolpman**
**Fiddlehead**
**Flying Goat**
Jalama

**LOMPOC**

**Loring Wine Co.**

Babcock    Melville

246

**Foley**

Ynez
Santa Rosa Rd

**D'Alfonso-Curran**

Sanford

*River*

Dierberg & Star Lane

Casa Cassara

**Lafond**

**Alma Rosa**

Mosby

**BUELLTON**

**SOLVANG**

**Hitching Post**

**Buttonwood Farm**
**Lincourt**

**Carr Vineya**

**SANTA YNEZ**

**Gair**

101

Alisal Rd

Refigio Rd

Point Arguello

Jalama Rd

1

Gaviota Pass

101

Point Conception

**GAVIOTA**

101

# SANTA BARBARA
# COUNTY WINERIES

# LOS OLIVOS AREA

0 — 1 Mile
0 — 1 Kilometer

to San Luis Obispo

154

101

Foxen Canyon Rd

Qupé
Carhartt
Alexander & Wayne
Arthur Earl
Scott Cellars
Epiphany
Daniel Gehrs
Carina Cellars
Longoria
Byron
Alamo  Pintado Ave
Presqu'ile  Tercero
Consilience & Tre Anelli  Dragonette
Blair Fox
Andrew Murray
Stolpman
Brander
Roblar Ave

**LOS OLIVOS**

Grand Ave
N Refugio Rd

Bridlewood

Roblar Ave

154

Beckmen

Ballard Canyon Rd

Blackjack Ranch

Roblar

Rd

**BALLARD**

Baseline Rd

Rusack

**Lincourt**

Refugio Rd

Edison

Rideau

Alamo Pintado Rd

**Buttonwood Farm**

to Santa Barbara

**Carr Vineyards**

**BUELLTON**

Ballard  Canyon  Rd

to Lompoc

Mission Dr

Chalk Hill Rd

246

**SANTA YNEZ**

Gainey

Santa Rosa Rd

Ave. of the Flags

**Hitching Post**

Shoestring

Lucas & Lewellen

Presidio

**SOLVANG**

Kalyra

Refugio Rd

101

to Santa Barbara

Royal Oaks

Toccata Tasting Room

Sunstone

figueroa tn

River

River

o San oaquin Valley

• **Featured Wineries**

• Other Wineries*

◯ CITIES AND TOWNS

*These selected wineries are shown for reference.
Most offer tastings or have tours; some receive
guests only by appointment or have limited hours.
Call ahead to verify hours of operation before visiting.

N

0 — 5 — 10 Miles
0 — 5 — 10 Kilometers

Cachuma Lake

154

*Santa Ynez River*

S a n t a   Y n e z   M o u n t a i n s

San Marcos Pass

154

ppy Canyon Rd

Happy Canyon/Margerum
Au Bon Climat
**Carr Vineyards**

**GOLETA**

101

217

University of
California
Santa Barbara

State

Foothill
Milpas
St

Rd  **MONTECITO**

**SUMMERLAND**

Jaffurs

Summerland

192

Santa Barbara
Winery

**SANTA
BARBARA**

**CARPINTERIA**

150

**OJAI**

SANTA BARBARA COUNTY

LOS ANGELES COUNTY

101

to Ventura and Los Angeles

*Santa   Barbara   Channel*

# ALMA ROSA WINERY & VINEYARDS

In the late 1960s, U.C. Berkeley geography graduate Richard Sanford returned from service in Vietnam yearning for a career far removed from the sadness of war. The prospect of growing Pinot Noir grapes intrigued him, and he embarked on a study of California climate data collected since 1900. The statistics revealed fascinating patterns in northern Santa Barbara County, where the unusual transverse mountain range runs east-west, funneling cool maritime air through the valleys to moderate the growing climate. Sanford was convinced that this part of the state could produce world-class Pinot Noir grapes to rival the best in France.

Sanford drove up and down the roads in the hills and valleys near Lompoc with an agricultural thermometer attached to his windshield and discovered temperature variations ideal for Pinot Noir in the Santa Rita Hills, where  grape growing was virtually unheard of at the time. In 1970 he cofounded the region's first Pinot Noir vineyard, Sanford & Benedict. In 1981 Sanford and his wife, Thekla, started Sanford Winery and a year later purchased the 700-acre Rancho El Jabalí (Ranch of the Wild Boar), part of the original mid-1800s Rancho Santa Rosa Mexican land grant. They planted the county's first certified organic vineyards and made balanced, elegant wines that garnered widespread international acclaim and helped establish Santa Rita Hills as an official appellation.

In 2005 the Sanfords separated from their namesake winery and began a new venture dedicated to organic farming and sustainable business practices, retaining Rancho El Jabalí, the tasting room, and a hundred-plus acres of certified organic vineyards. In Spanish, *alma* means "soul," and the name Alma Rosa embodies the Sanfords' philosophy that their wines reflect the soul of the historic rancho. Winemaker Alan Phillips focuses on continuing the Sanfords' reputation for excellence in Pinot Noir and Chardonnay, as well as small quantities of Pinot Gris, Pinot Blanc, and Pinot Noir Vin Gris, a dry rosé.

At El Jabalí, visitors can spot many species of birds and other wildlife. The long, gravel driveway winds through vineyards and sycamore groves, over a creek, up to the rustic tasting room—a converted tin-roofed 1920s dairy barn fashioned from pine planks. A pine tasting bar and cabinetry, red Spanish tile floor, original art by the Sanfords' friends, and bookcases filled with Richard's extensive collection of books lend the comfortable feeling of a Mexican hacienda to the interior. Outdoors, visitors unwind on the shaded stone patio, surrounded by stone flower boxes, a courtyard fountain, and groves of redwood trees, in sight of picnic tables above the spring-fed creek.

**ALMA ROSA WINERY & VINEYARDS**
7250 Santa Rosa Rd.
Buellton, CA 93427
805-688-9090
info@almarosawinery.com
www.almarosawinery.com

**OWNERS:** Richard and Thekla Sanford.

**LOCATION:** 5 miles west of U.S. 101 via Santa Rosa Rd. exit.

**APPELLATION:** Sta. Rita Hills.

**HOURS:** 11 A.M.–4:30 P.M. daily.

**TASTINGS:** $10 for 6 wines. Reservations required for groups of 8 or more.

**TOURS:** None.

**THE WINES:** Chardonnay, Pinot Blanc, Pinot Gris, Pinot Noir, Pinot Noir–Vin Gris.

**SPECIALTIES:** Chardonnay, Pinot Noir.

**WINEMAKER:** Alan Phillips.

**ANNUAL PRODUCTION:** 20,000 cases.

**OF SPECIAL NOTE:** Beautiful setting with creekside picnic area. Wildlife identification guides provided for visitor use in tasting room. Special premium bottlings available in tasting room.

**NEARBY ATTRACTIONS:** Historic Mission La Purísima; Nojoqui Falls County Park (hiking trails, picnic areas near seasonal waterfall).

# ANDREW MURRAY VINEYARDS

**ANDREW MURRAY VINEYARDS**
**TASTING ROOM**
2901-A Grand Ave.
Los Olivos, CA 93441
805-693-9644

**WINERY**
5095 Zaca Station Rd.
Los Olivos, CA 93441
805-686-9604
info@AndrewMurray
Vineyards.com
www.AndrewMurray
Vineyards.com

**OWNERS:** Andrew and
Kristen Murray.

**LOCATION:** Downtown Los
Olivos, one block south of
the intersection of Grand
Ave. and Hwy. 154.

**APPELLATION:** Santa Ynez
Valley.

**HOURS:** Tasting room:
11 A.M.–5 P.M. daily.
Winery: 11 A.M.–4 P.M.
Saturdays and Sundays,
April–mid-December.

**TASTINGS:** $10 for 6–8
wines.

**TOURS:** Of the winery,
11 A.M.–4 P.M. Saturday
and Sunday, and by
appointment.

**THE WINES:** Grenache,
Grenache Blanc,
Mourvèdre, Roussanne,
Syrah, Viognier.

**SPECIALTIES:** Rhône blends,
single-vineyard Syrahs

**WINEMAKER:**
Andrew Murray.

**ANNUAL PRODUCTION:**
6,000 cases.

**OF SPECIAL NOTE:** Periodic
special events, often co-
inciding with Los Olivos
holiday celebrations, at
tasting room. Covered terrace at winery with tables
for tastings and picnics.
Events at winery include
Vintner's Festival Open
House in April and Harvest
Party in the autumn.

**NEARBY ATTRACTION:**
Wildling Art Museum (art
of the American wilderness).

As a Southern California teenager, Andrew Murray yearned to be a rock musician. But a passion for winemaking detoured him while traveling through France's Rhône Valley in the late 1980s. Smitten with Syrah and Viognier, he abandoned his paleontology studies at U.C. Berkeley and channeled his creative ambitions in a new direction. He spent fifteen months in Australia, gaining valuable experience with Rhône varietals during a nine-month internship and subsequent stints at various vineyards and wineries. He returned to the United States to earn a degree in viticulture and enology from U.C. Davis and in 1990 founded Andrew Murray Vineyards in Santa Ynez, dedicated to Syrah and other Rhône varietals.

More than two decades later, Murray enjoys a reputation as a rock-star winemaker with distinctive, quality wines at surprisingly modest prices. He sources grapes from a collection of Santa Barbara County and other Central Coast vineyards with varying *terroir* and temperature ranges — cool, midrange, and warm. The broad array of fruit characteristics and flavors enables Murray to craft single-vineyard Syrahs as well as a number of provocative blends. His most notable single-vineyard Syrahs derive from Terra Bella Vineyard in Paso Robles, where warm days and cool nights yield an Australian Shiraz-style grape, and Watch Hill Vineyard in cool-climate Los Alamos, where grapes develop flavors reminiscent of authentic French Syrah. His most popular blends include Tous Les Jours, a Syrah blend for daily consumption; Esperance, a trio of Grenache, Syrah, and Mourvèdre in the style of great French red wines; and RGB, a white wine blend made from Roussanne and Grenache Blanc. Murray follows a philosophy akin to vinicultural *kaizen,* a Japanese term referring to continuous improvement. He constantly experiments with innovations, for example, trying unusual blends and screwcaps, and using rule-breaking methods to nurture subtle nuances from each vintage.

Visitors can taste the latest releases at the sleek tasting room in downtown Los Olivos, which mirrors Murray's minimalist, unassuming approach to winemaking. A four-decade music playlist livens up the space, which has a mahogany tasting bar, a comfy sofa, and gift displays. Out on the small front porch, tasters can relax and enjoy picnics with their wine.

On weekends Murray welcomes visitors to the hilltop winery in the San Rafael Mountains, about five miles north of downtown Los Olivos. A covered terrace overlooking vineyards provides a stellar setting for tastings and picnics. Intimate tours of the facility, often led by Murray, provide a wonderful opportunity to discover firsthand his passionate, rock 'n' roll style in the world of wine.

# BLAIR FOX CELLARS

The small town of Los Olivos looks much as it did in the late 1800s when the stagecoach stopped here to rest weary travelers and horses. A tall flagpole anchors the main intersection, and old Victorians and country cottages line the broad avenues. One such cottage, with rustic cedar siding, sits on a peaceful corner a short stroll from the flagpole. It houses a popular coffee shop, where locals gather to relax. It also holds the Blair Fox Cellars tasting room, where winemaker Blair Fox's limited-quantity, handcrafted Rhône wines take center stage.

Fox grew up in Santa Barbara and began pre-med studies at U.C. Santa Barbara. He transferred to U.C. Davis, where he took an enology class and found it so captivating that he switched career plans. Fox returned to Santa Barbara and enology, and a newfound passion for Syrah, Viognier, and other Rhône varieties. After winery for three years, Fox traveled through France's Rhône Valley and then worked as a winemaker in the McLaren Vale wine region in Australia. He returned to California in 2002, and Fess Parker Winery hired him to oversee the

Rhône wine production. In 2005 Fox became head winemaker of both Fess Parker Winery and its sister label, Epiphany. His talents quickly garnered him much praise and numerous accolades, including the coveted André Tchelistcheff Winemaker of the Year Award in 2008.

Fox still works at Fess Parker Winery, but crafts small-lot, vineyard-designated Syrah and other Rhône wines for his Blair Fox Cellars label. He sources most grapes from the all-organic, hand-farmed Fox Family Vineyard in Los Olivos, where vines thrive in ideal growing conditions: extreme hillsides with rocky, nutrient-poor soil. Other sources include the biodynamic Purisima Mountain Vineyard and sustainably farmed Tierra Alta Vineyard, both in Ballard Canyon, and Paradise Road Vineyard, whose warm climate results in particularly bold, flavorful fruit. Fox literally affixes his "thumbprints" through all phases of production, from punchdowns, racking, and bottling to disgorging sparkling wines.

Fox shares the results of his creative techniques in the cottage tasting room, which feels much like the winemaker's family home. Eclectic furnishings and art contribute to the warm, welcoming vibe. Fox often hangs out to chat with visitors, as does his wife, Sarah, who helps with all facets of the business, and their two young daughters, Rylee and Haylee. People can sit for a spell at the bar, hand-hewn from Australian white oak from a hundred-year-old Tasmanian schoolhouse, and sample Fox's latest releases—an opportunity available only in the tasting room and at special events.

**BLAIR FOX CELLARS**
2902-B San Marcos Ave.
Los Olivos, CA 93441
805-691-1678
info@blairfoxcellars.com
www.blairfoxcellars.com

**OWNERS:** Blair and Sarah Fox.

**LOCATION:** Downtown Los Olivos; front door is on Alamo Pintado Ave.

**APPELLATIONS:** All within Santa Barbara County.

**HOURS:** 12 P.M. – 5 P.M. Friday–Sunday, and by appointment.

**TASTINGS:** $12 for 5 wines (includes etched crystal glass).

**TOURS:** None.

**THE WINES:** Grenache, Petite Sirah, Syrah, Vermentino, Viognier.

**SPECIALTIES:** Vineyard-designated Syrahs, estate-grown Grenache, Syrah, Petite Sirah, and Vermentino.

**WINEMAKER:** Blair Fox.

**ANNUAL PRODUCTION:** 800 cases.

**OF SPECIAL NOTE:** Estate vineyard is organically grown and farmed entirely by hand without large mechanical equipment. Small, ultraboutique winery; wines available only in tasting room. Winemaker Blair Fox is often in the tasting room, pouring wine for guests.

**NEARBY ATTRACTIONS:** Wildling Art Museum (art of the American wilderness); historic buildings in Los Olivos and Ballard; Clairmont Farm Lavender Company; Quicksilver Miniature Horse Ranch.

# BUTTONWOOD FARM WINERY & VINEYARD

**BUTTONWOOD FARM WINERY & VINEYARD**
1500 Alamo Pintado Rd.
Solvang, CA 93463
805-688-3032
info@buttonwoodwinery.com
www.buttonwoodwinery.com

**OWNERS:** Bret C. Davenport, Seyburn Zorthian, Barry Zorthian.

**LOCATION:** 2 miles north of Hwy. 246.

**APPELLATION:** Santa Ynez Valley.

**HOURS:** 11 A.M.–5 P.M. daily.

**TASTINGS:** $10 for 5 wines (includes complimentary wineglass).

**TOURS:** None.

**THE WINES:** Cabernet Franc, Cabernet Sauvignon, dry Rosé, Grenache, Grenache Blanc, Malbec, Marsanne, Merlot, P.O.S.H. (port-style dessert wine), Sauvignon Blanc, Syrah, Trevin (Bordeaux blend).

**SPECIALTY:** Sauvignon Blanc.

**WINEMAKER:** Karen Steinwachs.

**ANNUAL PRODUCTION:** 8,500 cases.

**OF SPECIAL NOTE:** Winery hosts many special events, including Red, White, and Blues concert in June; peach celebration in July; All Buttonwood Farm dinner in August; and Pomegranate Festival and Holiday Open House in December. Fresh peach sales in July and August. Garden picnic area under buttonwood trees.

**NEARBY ATTRACTIONS:** Historic buildings in Los Olivos and Ballard; Clairmont Farm Lavender Company; Quicksilver Miniature Horse Ranch; Windhaven Glider Rides; historic Mission Santa Inés.

Scenic Alamo Pintado Road winds its way through a bucolic five-mile valley between Solvang and the village of Los Olivos. Buttonwood Farm, a working farm since the 1800s, occupies 106 acres in the heart of the valley. Much of the property remains an undisturbed wildlife ecosystem, and native buttonwood trees, also called sycamores, pepper the landscape. Orchards laden with peaches, pomegranates, pears, olives, and almonds and gardens filled with vegetables, herbs, and flowers surround the cottage-style tasting room visible from the roadside entrance.

Betty Williams, an avid equestrian, purchased Buttonwood Farm in 1968 to build a new home and develop a thoroughbred horse breeding and training facility. Williams felt strongly about preserving the local environment and cofounded the Land Trust for Santa Barbara County. In the early 1980s a vintner friend convinced her that the ancient riverbed would make an excellent vineyard site. In 1983 Williams and her son-in-law, Bret Davenport, started planting thirty-nine acres of sustainably farmed Bordeaux and Rhône-style grapes, and in 1989 completed a winery next to the vineyard. Her daughter and resident artist, Seyburn Zorthian, created label art influenced by studies with an abstract brushstroke master in Japan.

Since 1996 Buttonwood Farm's Sauvignon Blanc has attracted widespread acclaim, and Sauvignon Blanc continues to comprise more than a third of the winery's total production. In the early years, Buttonwood Farm sold most of its grapes to other Central Coast winemakers. After 1998 Buttonwood kept all of its estate fruit for its own wines. In 2007 Karen Steinwachs became head winemaker at Buttonwood. Steinwachs, a dropout from the tech world, had previously worked as assistant winemaker at Foley Estates Vineyard & Winery and at Fiddlehead Cellars. She has found her niche working with Buttonwood's estate vineyard, including new plantings of Grenache, Grenache Blanc, and Malbec.

Visitors to the casual, light-filled tasting room can sample recent Buttonwood Farm releases amid colorful floral arrangements—freshly cut from the garden—and displays of gifts and food items, including estate-grown peach preserves, tomatillo salsa, and dried herbs. Weather permitting, wine can be tasted outside on the patio. Guests are welcome to stroll the shale paths through the rambling gardens and relax in the shade of the buttonwood trees.

# CAMBRIA ESTATE WINERY

In the far northeast corner of Santa Barbara County, the Santa Maria Bench overlooks the ancient, gravelly banks of the Sisquoc River. The native Chumash called the area *tepuztli*, or "copper coin." Later, Spanish settlers called it Tepusquet (*tep*-us-kay). The steep slopes of the Tepusquet Mountains rise from the valley north of the bench, creating an unobstructed funnel for the cooling coastal breezes and fog that flow from the ocean seventeen miles to the west. In 1970 and 1971, pioneering Central Coast viticulturalist Louis Lucas and partners George Lucas and Alfred Gagnon planted Tepusquet Vineyard along this remarkable benchland, part of the 1838 Rancho Tepusquet Mexican land grant. The grapes thrived, and winemakers began to covet the fruit grown on the Santa Maria Bench for the rich, expressive character that the *terroir* imparts to cool-climate varieties such as Pinot Noir, Chardonnay, and Syrah.

In 1986 Barbara Banke, proprietor of several family-owned California wineries, purchased a portion of the original Tepusquet Vineyard. She established Cambria Estate Winery the next year to produce single-vineyard and small-block Chardonnays and Pinot Noirs, along with small quantities of Syrah and Viognier. Today Cambria Estate Winery occupies 1,600 southwest-facing acres and includes a winery, cellar, and tasting room. Banke named two of the four sustainably farmed estate vineyards after her daughters, Katherine and Julia; the other two include Tepusquet, in honor of the historic origins, and Bench Break, on the steepest slope above the estate.

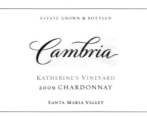

ESTATE GROWN & BOTTLED
*Cambria*
KATHERINE'S VINEYARD
2009 CHARDONNAY
SANTA MARIA VALLEY

Cambria has identified seventeen distinct soil types and many microclimates on the estate, and recently began replanting vineyard blocks to apply knowledge gained from more than two decades of experimentation. Many blocks are farmed and harvested individually according to their unique soils, microclimate, and elevation. Head winemaker Denise Shurtleff, who joined Cambria in 1999, crafts most of the handpicked estate grapes into nearly fifteen different bottlings. Pinot Noir grapes from Julia's Vineyard are sold to other wineries, including nearby Bonaccorsi, Foxen, and Hitching Post Wines.

A half-mile drive through the vineyards leads to Cambria's stone winery building. The tasting room, tucked in a corner on the top floor of the winery, was completely remodeled in 2006. Copper jugs and spittoons sit on a sleek, L-shaped brushed-concrete bar. An exhibit features photos of the barrel-making process. Glass windows enable visitors to observe winery operations in the barrel storage room below. Visitors can relax on the leather sofa before the fireplace and picnic on a nearby knoll with sweeping views of the Santa Maria Bench and Tepusquet Mountains.

**CAMBRIA ESTATE WINERY**
5475 Chardonnay Ln.
Santa Maria, CA 93454
805-938-7318
info@cambriawines.com
www.cambriawines.com

**OWNER:** Barbara Banke.

**LOCATION:** 12 miles east of downtown Santa Maria on the Foxen Trail.

**APPELLATION:** Santa Maria Valley.

**HOURS:** 10 A.M.–5 P.M. daily.

**TASTINGS:** $10 for 6 wines.

**TOURS:** By request.

**THE WINES:** Chardonnay, Pinot Gris, Pinot Noir, Syrah, Viognier.

**SPECIALTIES:** Estate-grown vineyard-designated Pinot Noirs and Chardonnays.

**WINEMAKER:** Denise Shurtleff.

**OF SPECIAL NOTE:** Gift shop with cookbooks, clothing, and small selection of deli foods. Small patio with tables adjacent to tasting room. Picnic area on knoll overlooking vineyards. Single-clone estate Chardonnays and Pinot Noirs, Pinot Gris, and Syrah available only in tasting room.

**NEARBY ATTRACTION:** Colson Canyon Road Mountain Bike and Hiking Trail.

# CARHARTT VINEYARD

**CARHARTT VINEYARD**
2990-A Grand Ave.
Los Olivos, CA 93441
805-693-5100
info@carharttvineyard.com
www.carharttvineyard.com

**OWNERS:** Mike and Brooke
Carhartt.

**LOCATION:** Just over
.25 mile from Hwy. 154.

**APPELLATION:** Santa Ynez
Valley.

**HOURS:** 11 A.M.–5 P.M. daily.

**TASTINGS:** $10 for 7 wines.

**TOURS:** None.

**THE WINES:** Merlot, Rosé,
Sangiovese, Sauvignon
Blanc, Syrah, Zinfandel.

**SPECIALTIES:** Estate Syrah,
Merlot, Rosé, Sangiovese.

**WINEMAKERS:** Brooke
and Mike Carhartt.

**ANNUAL PRODUCTION:**
3,000 cases.

**OF SPECIAL NOTE:** The
smallest tasting room in
the county. Owners pour
wine for guests.

**NEARBY ATTRACTIONS:**
Wildling Art Museum (art
of the American wilder-
ness); historic buildings
in Los Olivos and Ballard;
Clairmont Farm Lavender
Company; Quicksilver
Miniature Horse Ranch.

At the northern end of Grand Avenue, the main street in Los Olivos, sits an unassuming 1950s wooden cottage covered with climbing roses—the Carhartt Vineyard tasting room. Nearly everything here, indoors and out, reflects a sense of place—of deep connections to the land and people. Wooden tubs with flowers line the walkway and extend from the cottage down the block. On most days, owner Mike Carhartt welcomes visitors into the intimate space and, at the faux stone bar, proudly pours tastes of wines that he has handcrafted with his wife, Brooke. Behind the cottage, Japanese maples and a neighbor's pepper tree shade a cozy patio and garden.

The Carhartt connection to the Santa Ynez Valley took root long ago. A descendant of Hamilton Carhartt, founder of the famed Carhartt Overall Company, Mike grew up on the family's historic Rancho Santa Ynez, a large cattle and horse ranch. In 1993 he and Brooke acquired fifty acres of the former family estate. Mike had been around farming all of his life and had watched the valley develop into a premier wine region, so it made perfect sense for him to devote a portion of the ranch to wine grapes. In 1996 he and Brooke planted ten acres on a six-hundred-foot mesa with optimal conditions for growing Rhône and Bordeaux varietals: maximum sun exposure, warm afternoons, cool evenings, and sandy loam soil.

At first the Carhartts sold most of their fruit to other winemakers. They converted a hay barn into a winery, and Brooke studied enology. In 1998, the first year of fruit production, they vinified two barrels for their own label bearing the Carhartt cattle brand. These early Merlots and Syrahs garnered favorable reviews and awards, so they continued to develop their own program and soon had enough wine to open a tasting room. Their current estate plantings include Merlot, Syrah, Sauvignon Blanc, Petite Sirah, and Grenache; they also grow Sangiovese at neighboring Eleven Oaks Vineyard and purchase Cabernet Franc, Cabernet Sauvignon, and Zinfandel from other sources.

Although the Carhartts can be found in the tasting room, Brooke still manages all of the winemaking, and Mike spends part of every day in the vineyard. Their son, Chase, has completed his degree in viticulture and enology. As the third generation of Carhartts, he continues to expand his role in the family enterprise.

# CARR VINEYARDS & WINERY

arr Winery, in the heart of downtown Santa Barbara, ranks among the most distinctive tasting rooms in the region. The red and white Quonset hut, which resembles a wine cave, originally served as a military barracks at Santa Barbara Airport during World War II. In 2006 winemaker Ryan Carr seized the opportunity to open a new winery and tasting room in the hut, which offered everything he sought: ample space for winemaking operations (4,500 square feet), a downtown location, and easy access via walking, cycling, or public transportation.

Ryan and his wife, Jessica, who serves as director of sales and marketing, immediately began transforming the hut into an efficient winemaking operation and attractive tasting room. They added eco-friendly insulation, tasting bar made by hand from eye-catching works of art such as a a wineglass and a forty-five-pound Outside, a tiny patio with redwood shaded tables beckons visitors to door opens to a cool, cavernous oak and stainless steel wine barrels,

fashioned a striking wraparound wine barrels, and decorated with whimsical robot figurine clutching longboard Ryan built in college. Adirondack chairs and umbrella-stop and enter the winery. The room, where guests can view the play tabletop shuffleboard, and

listen to music while tasting Ryan's ultrapremium, limited-production wines. In the fall, visitors can watch Ryan and staff make and bottle wine in the same space.

Before launching his winemaking career, Ryan Carr studied plant science and majored in graphic design at the University of Arizona. After college, Carr headed to Santa Ynez, determined to build a career in winemaking. One of his first jobs was very hands-on—working in the fields for a local vineyard management company. In 1998 he was presented with the opportunity to make wine for Stolpman Vineyards at Central Coast Wine Services. A year later, he produced his first vintage—a total of ten cases—using grapes from a vineyard where he worked. The success of this initial effort inspired him to establish his own vineyard development company and winery.

Today Carr Vineyards supervises more than a hundred acres of vineyards throughout Santa Barbara County, including Paredon (Syrah and Grenache), Morehouse (Syrah), Susich (Syrah), Turner (Pinot Noir, Syrah, and Pinot Gris), and Kessler-Haak (Pinot Noir and Chardonnay). All Carr wines are made from Santa Barbara County grapes grown to Ryan Carr's exact specifications. He now specializes in Pinot Noir, Pinot Gris, and Cabernet Franc. Carr is a big fan of Grenache, but produces it in extremely limited quantities. He spends much of his time outdoors in the vineyards, but often stops by the winery to chat with visitors about his latest vintages.

**CARR VINEYARDS & WINERY**
414 N. Salsipuedes St.
Santa Barbara, CA 93103
805-965-7985
info@carrwinery.com
www.carrwinery.com

**OWNER:** Ryan Carr.

**LOCATION:** 6 blocks east of State St. at E. Gutierrez St.

**APPELLATIONS:** Happy Canyon of Santa Barbara, Santa Ynez Valley, Sta. Rita Hills.

**HOURS:** 11 A.M.–6 P.M. Sunday–Wednesday; 11 A.M.–8 P.M. Thursday–Saturday.

**TASTINGS:** $10. Reservations requested for 8 or more guests. $12 tasting fee for groups over 20.

**TOURS:** None.

**THE WINES:** Cabernet Franc, Grenache, Pinot Gris, Pinot Noir, Sangiovese, Syrah.

**SPECIALTIES:** Cabernet Franc, Pinot Gris, Pinot Noir.

**WINEMAKER:** Ryan Carr.

**ANNUAL PRODUCTION:** 3,500 cases.

**OF SPECIAL NOTE:** Wines by the glass, flights of wine, wine on tap, and tastings offered daily. Winemaker dinner, art shows, and other special events scheduled year-round. The winery has a second tasting room in Santa Ynez.

**NEARBY ATTRACTIONS:** East Beach and Cabrillo Bathhouse (city of Santa Barbara's main beach); Santa Barbara Zoo; Santa Barbara Waterfront District; historic Mission Santa Barbara; Santa Barbara Museum of Art.

# COSTA DE ORO WINERY

**COSTA DE ORO WINERY**
1331 S. Nicholson Ave.
Santa Maria, CA 93454
805-922-1468
info@cdowinery.com
www.cdowinery.com

**OWNERS:** Burk and
Espinola families.

**LOCATION:** Just east of U.S.
101 at Stowell Rd. exit.

**APPELLATION:** Santa Maria
Valley.

**HOURS:** 11 A.M.–6 P.M. daily
plus Friday evening Wine
Down 5–8 P.M.

**TASTINGS:** $10 for 5 wines.

**TOURS:** None.

**THE WINES:** Cabernet
Sauvignon, Chardonnay,
Merlot, Pinot Grigio, Pinot
Noir, Sauvignon Blanc,
Syrah, Tempranillo.

**SPECIALTIES:** Estate
Chardonnay and
Pinot Noir.

**WINEMAKER:** Gary Burk.

**ANNUAL PRODUCTION:**
6,500 cases.

**OF SPECIAL NOTE:** Pet
friendly. Deli case with
cheeses, meats, and crackers. Large gift shop with
wine-themed items, books,
and local arts and crafts.
On-site patio and picnic
area. Lounge area. Friday
Night Wine Down with live
music, wines by the glass,
and appetizers. Cabernet
Sauvignon, Sauvignon
Blanc, Syrah, Rosé, Merlot,
and Pinot Grigio available
only in tasting room.

**NEARBY ATTRACTIONS:** Pacific
Conservatory of the Per-
forming Arts (year-round
theater performances);
Santa Maria Museum
of Flight; Dunes Center
(exhibits on Guadalupe-
Nipomo Dunes Preserve).

Every Friday evening, local Santa Marians and visitors in the know head to the Costa de Oro Winery tasting room to celebrate the end of the workweek—and to launch the weekend in spirited style. They relax in the comfortable lounge, where they order appetizers and fine wines by the glass and bottle. They also listen to live music, ranging from rock to country and western, performed by various artists, including local Grammy Award winners and touring groups.

This unusual, beyond-the-bottle blend of music and wine reflects the dual passions of Costa de Oro winemaker/musician Gary Burk. His father, Ron Burk, and Bob Espinola founded Gold Coast Farms in 1978 in the heart of the Santa Maria Valley. Fruits and vegetables thrived there, except on a particular bluff—Fuglar's

Point. The farmers had a hunch that the bluff's well-drained, sandy loam soil, a poor match for vegetables, would make an ideal home for wine grapes. In 1989 the Burk and Espinola families planted thirty acres, twenty to Pinot Noir and ten to Chardonnay, with vine cuttings from the famed Sierra Madre Vineyard just a few miles away.

The hunch proved correct. Gold Coast Vineyard began producing fruit in the early 1990s. Gary Burk, a singer and guitarist, lived in Los Angeles at the time. He supplemented his performance income by selling Gold Coast Vineyard grapes to Au Bon Climat, Foxen, and other local wineries. In 1994 Jim Clendenen, owner/winemaker at Au Bon Climat, and Bob Lindquist, owner/winemaker at Qupé winery at Bien Nacido Vineyards, offered Gary an assistant winemaking position. Gary accepted and simultaneously started producing the first Costa de Oro wines—one barrel each of Pinot Noir and Chardonnay. Gary stayed at Au Bon Climat and Qupé until 2002, when he left to devote his full energies to Costa de Oro. His award-winning wines, praised for their European-style elegance and balance, focus almost exclusively on Pinot Noir and Chardonnay made from estate fruit and other Santa Maria Valley grapes. Gary also sources fruit from other Central Coast vineyards and crafts wines at a shared facility in Santa Maria. Costa de Oro also produces specially bottled vintages for Roy's restaurants and for the Halekulani, a luxury hotel in Hawaii.

The casual, Tuscan-style Costa de Oro tasting room, opened in 2006, includes a tasting bar, plus sofa seating and tables for lounging. Windows open up to expansive views across Santa Maria Valley. Gift items and gourmet foods line the wooden tables and display cases. The room provides a warm, comfortable setting for tasting throughout the day, but becomes an extra-special venue on Friday nights, when wine, music, and good times with friends fill the air.

# D'ALFONSO-CURRAN WINES

**D'ALFONSO-CURRAN WINES**
4457 Santa Rosa Rd., Ste. 5
Lompoc, CA 93436
805-736-9463
info@d-cwines.com
www.d-cwines.com

**OWNERS:** Kris Curran, Bruno D'Alfonso.

**LOCATION:** 10 miles west of U.S. 101 via Santa Rosa Rd.

**APPELLATIONS:** Sta. Rita Hills, Santa Ynez Valley.

**HOURS:** Strictly by appointment.

**TASTINGS:** Custom-tailored to visitors' wishes.

**TOURS:** By appointment.

**THE WINES:** Chardonnay, Grenache, Grenache Blanc, Grenache Rosé (dry), Merlot, Nebbiolo, Pinot Grigio, Pinot Noir, Sangiovese, Tempranillo.

**SPECIALTIES:** Vineyard-designated Pinot Noirs and . Chardonnays, vineyard-designated Syrahs, Spanish varietals.

**WINEMAKERS:** Kris Curran, Bruno D'Alfonso.

**ANNUAL PRODUCTION:** 5,000 cases.

**OF SPECIAL NOTE:** Depending on the winery operations, it may be possible to arrange a tasting hosted by the winemakers. The winemakers also partner with guest chefs for events such as cooking demonstration classes with wine pairings at various venues throughout the region. Current schedule is on winery website.

**NEARBY ATTRACTIONS:** Historic Mission La Purísima; Nojoqui Falls County Park (hiking trails, picnic areas near seasonal waterfall); Santa Ynez Valley Farms (organic farm stand and petting zoo).

Rural, two-lane Santa Rosa Road meanders sixteen miles through the pastoral Sta. Rita Hills appellation, following the Santa Ynez River on its westward run to the Pacific Ocean. It's one of the area's most scenic settings, home to centuries-old ranches, ancient Chumash encampments, farms, and deer and other wildlife. A twenty minute drive west leads to historic Rancho La Viña. Once part of a vast Mexican land grant and family owned and operated since the 1860s, the 2,800-acre estate produces quality Pinot Noir grapes, walnuts, organic heirloom tomatoes, and other crops that thrive in the appellation's exceptional growing conditions. It also provides a home and custom winery facility for Bruno D'Alfonso and Kris Curran — names synonymous with world-class winemaking in Santa Barbara County.

D'Alfonso worked from 1983 to 2004 as head winemaker at Sanford Winery in Lompoc, where he crafted internationally acclaimed vintages. Curran met D'Alfonso in the early 1990s, worked at his side during crush, and quickly developed a passion for winemaking. In 2000 she was tapped as head winemaker at Sea Smoke Cellars, also in the Santa Rita Hills, where she created some of the nation's most sought-after Pinot Noirs. Eight years later, she was lured away to direct winemaking at Foley Estates Vineyard & Winery.

Today the husband-and-wife team focuses exclusively on their own collection of fine wines under four different labels. Wines bearing the D'Alfonso-Curran label showcase ultra-premium, vineyard-designated Pinot Noirs exclusively from the Santa Rita Hills and Chardonnays. Di Bruno vintages celebrate Bruno D'Alfonso's heritage with red and white Italian varieties (Pinot Grigio, Sangiovese, Nebbiolo, and Merlot). The Curran label concentrates on vineyard-designated Grenache, Grenache Gris, Grenache Blanc, and Tempranillo, as well as some Syrahs. BADGE wines feature blended Pinot Noirs and stainless steel Chardonnay.

A visit to the D'Alfonso-Curran winery facility at Rancho La Viña represents a rare opportunity to experience the hands-on, inner workings of a boutique, limited-production winery with expert guides: the winemakers themselves, accompanied by their beloved German shepherds. The pair, along with a small crew, perform all stages of wine production. They offer visits and vineyard tours by appointment only and tailor the schedule around winery operations that day, as well as visitors' particular interests. D'Alfonso and Curran often share advice on pairing wines with an array of cuisines. They are also known to regale guests with friendly banter as they explain — and demonstrate — their winemaking methods, widely acknowledged as some of the best in the business.

# FOLEY ESTATES VINEYARD & WINERY

**FOLEY ESTATES VINEYARD & WINERY**
6121 Hwy. 246
Lompoc, CA 93436
805-737-6222
tastingroom@foleywines.com
www.foleywines.com

**OWNER:** William Foley II.

**LOCATION:** 8 miles west of Buellton on Hwy. 246.

**APPELLATION:** Sta. Rita Hills.

**HOURS:** 10 A.M.–5 P.M. daily.

**TASTINGS:** $10 for 5 wines.

**TOURS:** None.

**THE WINES:** Chardonnay, Pinot Noir, Rosé, Syrah.

**SPECIALTIES:** Estate-grown Pinot Noir and Chardonnay from specific vineyard blocks.

**WINEMAKER:** Leslie Mead Renaud.

**ANNUAL PRODUCTION:** 40,000 cases.

**OF SPECIAL NOTE:** Picnic areas on-site, some under patio awning. Well-stocked gift shop with clothing, books, gourmet food items, and wine-themed crafts. Certain block-designated Chardonnay and Pinot Noir vintages available only in tasting room.

**NEARBY ATTRACTIONS:** Historic Mission La Purísima; Old Town Lompoc Heritage Walk (1-mile scenic tour with 18 stops); Jalama Beach County Park (tidepooling, nature trails, camping, surfing).

Along Highway 246 between Lompoc and Buellton, a stunning scene leaps into view from the roadside: a series of fifty-nine vineyard blocks blanketing steep, south-facing hillsides and the gently sloping valley below. The setting is Rancho Santa Rosa, home of Foley Estates Vineyard & Winery and part of the original 15,000-acre parcel granted by the Mexican government to former Presidio officer Francisco Cota's ten children in 1845.

Vintner Bill Foley, owner of Lincourt Vineyards in the Santa Ynez Valley since 1994, had successfully produced varietals suited for the region's warm climate. However, he hoped to establish a separate vineyard estate to focus on Pinot Noir, Chardonnay, Syrah, and other varietals that would thrive in the limestone soils and cooling maritime effects of the Sta. Rita Hills appellation. In 1998, with topographical maps and data from extensive soil and climate research in hand, he scoured the region and discovered an ideal site—the 460-acre Rancho Santa Rosa, with elevations from 500 to 1,000 feet above sea level. He then launched an ambitious project patterned after practices common in Burgundy's Côtes d'Or. He divided 230 acres of planted vines into fifty-nine small blocks (average size less than four acres), each farmed, harvested, and vinified separately according to specifications unique to the particular soils, microclimate, and elevation. Foley refurbished former stables to house a 12,000-square-foot, state-of-the-art winery, and completed an adjacent 3,500-square-foot tasting room and event center in 2005.

The Foley Estates Burgundian-influenced wines, highly regarded by wine critics and sommeliers, are known for their diversity and rich character. Estate vineyard blocks now include Pinot Noir, Syrah, Cinsault, Pinot Gris, Grenache, Grüner Veiltiner, Gewürztraminer, and Pinot Grigio. Vintner Leslie Mead Renaud uses her extensive hands-on experience to transform the fruit into sought-after wines. She honed her skills at several Northern California wineries, including Clos du Bois and Bonny Doon Vineyard, and at Talley Vineyards in the Edna Valley, where she was named head winemaker in 2007. In 2010 she joined Foley Family Wines as director of winemaking for Foley Estates and sister winery Lincourt.

The tasting room, in the spacious hospitality center, reflects the ranch's historic Spanish/Mexican roots in contemporary mission style, with light wood floors, a curved cherrywood tasting bar, and shelves displaying myriad items for purchase. Guests can sink into leather armchairs near a stone fireplace and enjoy the magnificent views of the surrounding oak-studded hills and multifaceted vineyard that defines the modern Rancho Santa Rosa.

# FOXEN

Friends for more than thirty years, Dick Doré and Bill Wathen forged the successful partnership behind Foxen and foxen 7200. Widely known as the Foxen Boys, the two began making wine together in 1985 with borrowed tools and Cabernet Sauvignon grapes from a Santa Maria vineyard. For twenty-four years, they crafted wine in a nearly two-hundred-year-old hay barn on Rancho Tinaquaic, originally an 8,874-acre Mexican land grant purchased by Doré's great-great-grandfather, Benjamin Foxen, in 1837. On weekends, they took turns running the tasting room in the family's weathered shack along the road. As they expanded their Bordeaux-based portfolio to include Rhône-, Burgundy-, and Cal-ifornia-style wines, they earned a reputation for exquisite quality and irreverent fun.

The winemaking operation eventually outgrew the old barn, and in 2009 Doré and Wathen opened a new solar-powered tasting room and winery down the road from their historic tasting shack. Sided with earth-toned redwood, the buildings resemble western barns and have monitor-style roofs for added light and air flow. Mounted on the warehouse roof, 216 solar panels provide nearly all of the facility's energy needs. Dense plantings of native California species flourish in wide beds and a bio-swale that nearly surrounds the property.

A textured concrete path leads to the tasting room entryway. Beyond the French doors, open beams of knotty pine and double-hung oak-framed windows confirm the country theme. At two L-shaped tasting bars—clad with corrugated tin and topped with polished concrete counters—staff members pour Foxen Chardonnay, Pinot Noir, and Rhône-style wines. Out back, visitors can relax at café-style tables. Views of the canyon include the grass-covered hills of Rancho Tinaquaic, settled by Benjamin Foxen. An English sea captain, he branded his livestock with a nautical design that inspired the winery's distinctive anchor-shaped logo.

A few yards south of the patio, the estate's sustainably and dry-farmed Tinaquaic "Bajita" Vineyard, planted in 2008, supports six acres of Syrah, Cabernet Franc, and Petit Verdot. The winery's original estate Tinaquaic Vineyard was planted in 1989 and, along with the new "Bajita" blocks, is the only dry-farmed vineyard in Santa Barbara County. Its eleven acres, comprised of Chardonnay, Cabernet Franc, and Syrah, are on a hilltop opposite the original tasting room, now known as foxen 7200. Once a blacksmith shop serving nineteenth-century stagecoaches, the rustic shack features the Foxen Boys' Bordeaux-style and blended Cal-Italian wines. It boasts wall-sized sliding doors that open to the rolling hills of Rancho Tinaquaic, which is still owned by Doré's family.

**FOXEN**
7600 Foxen Canyon Rd.
Santa Maria, CA 93454

**FOXEN 7200**
7200 Foxen Canyon Rd.
Santa Maria, CA 93454
805-937-4251
info@foxenvineyard.com
www.foxenvineyard.com

**OWNERS:** Bill Wathen, Richard Doré.

**LOCATION:** 16 miles north of the intersection of Hwy. 154 and Foxen Canyon Rd.

**APPELLATIONS:** Happy Canyon of Santa Barbara, Santa Maria Valley, Sta. Rita Hills.

**HOURS:** 11 A.M.–4 P.M. daily.

**TASTINGS:** $10 for 5 wines; $12 for 3 wines at each tasting room.

**TOURS:** None.

**THE WINES:** Chardonnay, Chenin Blanc, Grenache, Mourvèdre, Pinot Noir, Syrah (Foxen); Cabernet Franc, Cabernet Sauvignon, Merlot, Sangiovese, Sauvignon Blanc (foxen 7200).

**SPECIALTIES:** Single-vineyard, small-production wines. Foxen: Cuvée Jeanne Marie (Rhône-style blend); foxen 7200: Volpino (Cabernet Sauvignon/Merlot blend).

**WINEMAKER:** Bill Wathen.

**ANNUAL PRODUCTION:** 13,000 cases.

**OF SPECIAL NOTE:** Chardonnay Bien Nacido "Steel Cut," Sauvignon Blanc, and Mission (dessert wine) sold in tasting rooms only. Reservations required for groups larger than 6. Picnic tables on-site.

**NEARBY ATTRACTION:** Historic 1875 San Ramon Chapel (Benjamin Foxen Memorial Chapel).

# GAINEY VINEYARD

**GAINEY VINEYARD**
3950 E. Hwy. 246
Santa Ynez, CA 93460
805-688-0558
info@gaineyvineyard.com
www.gaineyvineyard.com

**OWNER:** Dan H. Gainey.

**LOCATION:** Off Hwy. 246,
.5 mile west of Hwy. 154.

**APPELLATIONS:** Santa Ynez
Valley, Sta. Rita Hills.

**HOURS:** 10 A.M.–5 P.M. daily.

**TASTINGS:** $10 for 6 wines;
$20 for 9 reserve wines.

**TOURS:** 11 A.M., 1 P.M.,
2 P.M., and 3 P.M. daily.
Appointment necessary
for groups of 8 or more.

**THE WINES:** Cabernet
Sauvignon, Chardon-
nay, Merlot, Pinot Noir,
Riesling, Sauvignon Blanc,
Syrah.

**SPECIALTIES:** Limited-
production wines from
selected vineyards.

**WINEMAKER:** Jeff LeBard.

**ANNUAL PRODUCTION:**
30,000 cases.

**OF SPECIAL NOTE:** Open
house during Santa
Barbara County Vintner's
Festival (weekends in April
and October). Annual
Crush Party (September).
Deli items sold on-site.
Limited Selection wines
available only in tasting
room.

**NEARBY ATTRACTIONS:**
Windhaven Glider
Rides; historic Mission
Santa Inés; Santa Ynez
Valley Historical Society
Museum (early California
exhibits, carriage house,
gift shop); Cachuma Lake
(county park with boating,
fishing, nature cruises).

The vast Gainey Ranch epitomizes the Santa Ynez Valley lifestyle, where farming, ranching, and equestrian pursuits go in tandem. In 1962 hardy Minnesotans Dan C. Gainey and his son Dan J. purchased 1,800 acres stretching along the banks of the Santa Ynez River and into the foothills. They continued to run an existing cattle business and launched a large-scale farming operation. In the early 1980s, Dan J. and his son Dan H. foresaw the potential to produce quality grapes. In 1983 they planted a fifty-acre vineyard. In 1984 they constructed a Spanish-style winery, designing it with the visitor in mind, at a time when the valley had few tasting rooms.

Today thousands of visitors come annually, not just to taste Gainey wines, but to witness life on a diverse working ranch. Cattle roam nearly a thousand acres on the oak-studded slopes of the Santa Ynez Mountains. More  than six hundred acres are devoted to a range of crops: alfalfa and forage grasses, organic vegetables (such as peppers, squash, broccoli, pumpkin, onions) and fruits (occasionally melons), and flowers for seed. An Arabian horse breeding and training facility occupies about a hun- dred acres of the estate. Grapes are grown on about a hundred acres at the Home Ranch in Santa Ynez, and more than a hundred acres at Evans Ranch (named for Dan H.'s great-grandfather) and another holding in the Santa Rita Hills — all distinct microclimates that provide the chance to grow many different varieties.

The Home Ranch vineyards are planted in Bordeaux varieties that tend to thrive in warmer conditions: Sauvignon Blanc, Merlot, Cabernet Sauvignon, and Cabernet Franc. The Santa Rita Hills vineyards, where temperatures average fifteen to twenty degrees cooler than the valley, focus on Chardonnay, Pinot Noir, and Syrah. Winemaker Jeff LeBard, a Central Coast native with more than a decade of experience crafting regional wines, transforms grapes from the estate vineyards into creative new vintages. Gainey Vineyard's Limited Selection wines, made from specific vineyard sections groomed to produce low yields and intense flavors, receive consistent critical praise. These typically feature Sauvignon Blanc, Chardonnay, Pinot Noir, Syrah, and several Bordeaux.

A visit to Gainey Vineyard should always be timed to include one of the popular, comprehensive tours of the gravity-flow winery. The hospitality center resembles a Spanish-style hacienda, with wooden benches and doors, wrought-iron embellishments, Spanish tile floors, and high-beamed ceilings. Outdoors, pepper trees line the long entrance drive that leads to an expansive lawn with tables and an arbor-shaded veranda — excellent spots for a picnic and observing ranch life firsthand.

# HITCHING POST WINES

It's one thing to pair wines with food. But how many chefs crush, barrel, and bottle the wine served with the food they prepare? Chef-winemaker Frank Ostini set out to accomplish just that in 1979. His parents had operated the popular Hitching Post steak house in Casmalia, near Santa Maria, since 1952. They specialized in Santa Maria–style barbecue—grilling steaks and chops over an open fire of red oak. After Ostini returned from college in 1976, he worked in the Hitching Post kitchen. As a lark, he decided to create his own wines to complement the restaurant's meals. He asked a friend, Gray Hartley, to join him in the backyard project. Hartley agreed, and the duo made a Merlot in an old  whiskey barrel. The next year, they produced a Cabernet, fol-lowed in 1981 by a Pinot Noir. Pleased with the results of their amateur Pinot Noir, a variety that had not yet emerged as a regional star, Ostini and Hartley went commercial in 1984 and soon gained critical acclaim for smooth vintages that matched extremely well with food.

In 1991 Hartley and Ostini produced enough wine to sell outside the restaurant. Because Hartley fished commercially in Alaska for more than twenty years, his seafaring days have influenced some of the winery's signature labels: the flagship Highliner Pinot Noir uses a term that refers to the best fisherman in the fleet. Hartley and Ostini give credit to the sources for their wines: prestigious vineyards throughout Santa Barbara County, including Julia's Vineyard, Bien Nacido, Fiddlestix, and Cargasacchi.

Ostini opened the Hitching Post II restaurant in Buellton in 1986. He retained the Santa Maria–style barbecue, but added eclectic ingredients such as quail and duck to the menu. Flights of Hitching Post wines are available for tasting in the wood-paneled lounge area. Bartenders pour the wine samples, and many visitors also order from the appetizer menu. The movie *Sideways* was filmed extensively at the restaurant in 2003, and photos of Ostini and the cast line the walls.

In 2008 Hartley and Ostini moved their winemaking operations from Santa Maria to Terravant Wine Company, a custom winemaking facility in Buellton. Although tastings of Hitching Post wines are offered at Terravant's new visitor center, wine aficionados continue to flock to the ever-popular Hitching Post II, where the chef-winemaker blends his culinary and vinous creations.

**HITCHING POST WINES**
The Hitching Post II
406 E. Hwy. 246
Buellton, CA 93427
805-688-0676
info@hitchingpostwines.com
www.hpwines.com

**OWNER:** Frank Ostini.

**LOCATION:** 1 mile east of U.S. 101.

**APPELLATIONS:** Santa Maria Valley, Santa Ynez Valley, Sta. Rita Hills.

**HOURS:** 4–6 P.M. Monday–Friday; 3–5 P.M. Saturday and Sunday (for wine tasting).

**TASTINGS:** $9 for 6 wines.

**TOURS:** None.

**THE WINES:** Cabernet Franc, Merlot, Pinot Noir, Rosé, Syrah.

**SPECIALTY:** Highliner Pinot Noir.

**WINEMAKERS:** Gray Hartley, Frank Ostini.

**ANNUAL PRODUCTION:** 11,000 cases.

**OF SPECIAL NOTE:** Tastings are held in one of the most popular restaurants in the Santa Ynez Valley. Wines are made by chef-owner to complement menu.

**NEARBY ATTRACTIONS:** Ostrich Land (33-acre ostrich farm); Elverhøj Museum of History and Art (exhibits on Danish community in Solvang); Windhaven Glider Rides; historic Mission Santa Inés.

# LAFOND WINERY & VINEYARDS

**LAFOND WINERY & VINEYARDS**
6855 Santa Rosa Rd.
Buellton, CA 93427
805-688-7921
rr@lafondwinery.com
www.lafondwinery.com

**OWNER:** Pierre Lafond.

**LOCATION:** 5.5 miles west of U.S. 101 at Buellton.

**APPELLATION:** Sta. Rita Hills.

**HOURS:** 10 A.M.–5 P.M. daily.

**TASTINGS:** $5 for 6 wines; $10 on weekends.

**TOURS:** None.

**THE WINES:** Chardonnay, Grenache, Pinot Noir, Riesling, Syrah.

**SPECIALTY:** Pinot Noir.

**WINEMAKER:** Bruce McGuire.

**ANNUAL PRODUCTION:** 6,000–8,000 cases.

**OF SPECIAL NOTE:** Pet-friendly, expansive grounds with lawns and picnic areas; extensive gift shop. Open house for Vintner's Festival (April) and Harvest Festival (October). Many wines available only in tasting room.

**NEARBY ATTRACTIONS:** Historic Mission La Purísima; Nojoqui Falls County Park (hiking trails, picnic areas near seasonal waterfall); Santa Ynez Valley Farms (organic farm stand and petting zoo).

Few wineries can claim roots as deep in Santa Barbara County soil as Lafond Winery & Vineyards. Architect Pierre Lafond moved from Canada to Santa Barbara in 1957. He opened a wine and cheese shop and decided to wed two of his greatest passions, wine and business, by entering the winemaking industry. In 1962 he founded Santa Barbara Winery—the first winery in Santa Barbara County to open since Prohibition. Local wine grapes were not readily available at the time, so Lafond had to purchase fruit from San Luis Obispo County for nearly a decade. Set on growing his own grapes to control availability and quality, he purchased 105 acres in the Santa Rita Hills, along the banks  of the Santa Ynez River, and established the 65-acre Lafond Vineyards in 1971. In 1996 Lafond purchased additional property across the river and planted 30 acres of Pinot Noir and Syrah. In 2009 he added 37 leased acres from neighboring Burning Creek Ranch and began planting Pinot Noir from eight selected clones.

Bruce McGuire, a pioneer in the development of Pinot Noir and Syrah in California, has been winemaker for Lafond Winery and Santa Barbara Winery since 1981. He produces wines in small lots for both labels. However, he crafts most Lafond Winery wines with exceptional lots of Pinot Noir, Syrah, and Chardonnay grapes exclusively from the Santa Rita Hills, often from particular vineyard blocks differentiated by soil quality and vigor. David Lafond, Pierre's son, manages the winery and vineyards, employing sustainable practices such as riding a horse through the vineyards to test grapes and recycling grape pumice as landscape decoration. Pierre's daughter, Michelle Lafond, serves as marketing director.

The Lafond Winery & Vineyards tasting room, designed by Pierre Lafond and constructed by David Lafond, opened in 2001. Rich mahogany details, including a custom-made bar and wine display cases, reign throughout the contemporary Mediterranean-style tasting room. Pierre Lafond and his wife, Wendy Foster, operate several enterprises in Santa Barbara, including clothing stores, bistros, and gourmet markets. Many items found in those businesses line shelves and tables in the well-stocked winery gift shop: works by local artisans, oils, vinegars, clothing, books, and gourmet foods. Glass doors open to the winemaking facility and barrel room, allowing visitors a bird's-eye view of winemaking operations. Out back, a patio with grapevines, arbors, and olive trees is used for hosting special events. Visitors are invited to stroll through the scenic grounds, which include pine and olive groves, ponds, and expansive lawns with picnic areas overlooking the storied vineyards—planted in the earliest days of the region's winegrowing history.

# LINCOURT WINERY

I t's virtually impossible to miss Lincourt Winery's tasting room in the heart of the Santa Ynez Valley. A century-old windmill stands tall amid rows of vineyards and remains as testament to the property's historic traditions as a dairy farm back in the 1800s. Many a marriage proposal takes place beneath the iconic structure, which is surrounded by sprawling grounds sprinkled with California pepper trees.

Financier and vintner Bill Foley founded Lincourt Winery soon after he and his wife, Carol, had relocated their family to Santa Barbara in 1994. A longtime fan of Burgundian wines, Foley discovered that the winegrowing region just a few miles north of his home had the potential to produce exceptional Pinot Noir and  Chardonnay. Foley hired renowned winemaker Alan Phillips to help him secure vineyard sites and spearhead his dream of producing benchmark regional wines. In 1996 the Foleys purchased the historic farm, which included two of the valley's oldest vineyards, Alamo Pintado and La Cuesta, planted in 1972. They named their new winery Lincourt, a fusion of their daughters' names, Lindsay and Courtney. The Foleys later established Foley Estates.

Leslie Mead Renaud came aboard as Lincourt's winemaker in 2010, bringing extensive experience from positions at Bonny Doon Vineyard in Santa Cruz County and Talley Vineyards in San Luis Obispo County. She handcrafts premium Chardonnay, Pinot Noir, Sauvignon Blanc, and other Burgundian-style wines at the state-of-the-art Foley Estates facility. Grapes are grown at the twenty-four-acre Lincourt Winery property, Foley Estates, and Firestone Vineyards. Small-lot bottlings of Pinot Noir and Chardonnay bear the names of influential women in Bill Foley's life, and all labels show the image of Lincourt's famed windmill.

A visit to the winery resembles an old-fashioned outing to a neighbor's country home. A gravel driveway leads up a gentle slope through the vineyards to a 1926 bungalow. Guests sample Lincourt's latest vintages at tasting bars set up in a former dining room, breakfast room, and bedroom. Guests are welcome to relax and picnic ooutdoors on porches and a covered veranda. Country music plays softly in the background, enhancing the serene views of vineyards and the historic windmill below.

**LINCOURT WINERY**
1711 Alamo Pintado Rd.
Solvang, CA 93463
805-688-8554
tastingroom@
lincourtwines.com
www.lincourtwines.com

**OWNER:** Bill Foley.

**LOCATION:** On rural Alamo Pintado Rd., between the towns of Solvang and Los Olivos.

**APPELLATIONS:** Sta. Rita Hills, Santa Ynez Valley,

**HOURS:** 10 A.M.–5 P.M. daily.

**TASTINGS:** $10 for 6 wines.

**TOURS:** None.

**THE WINES:** Cabernet Sauvignon, Chardonnay, Merlot, Pinot Blanc, Pinot Grigio, Pinot Noir, Sauvignon Blanc, Syrah.

**SPECIALTIES:** Pinot Noir and Chardonnay.

**WINEMAKER:** Leslie Mead Renaud.

**ANNUAL PRODUCTION:** 40,000 cases.

**OF SPECIAL NOTE:** Cookbooks and wine-themed items sold in tasting room. Special events at the winery are listed on the website. Annie Dyer and Willie Mae Pinot Noir wines, and Carol Ann and Zoula Nunn Chardonnay wines available only in tasting room.

**NEARBY ATTRACTIONS:** Wildling Art Museum (art of the American wilderness); historic buildings in Los Olivos and Ballard; Clairmont Farm Lavender Company; Quicksilver Miniature Horse Ranch.

# LORING WINE COMPANY

**LORING WINE COMPANY**
1591 E. Chestnut Ave.
Lompoc, CA 93436
805-742-0478
Brian@LoringWine
Company.com
www.LoringWine
Company.com

**OWNERS:** Brian Loring and
Kimberly Loring.

**LOCATION:** Lompoc Wine
Ghetto, .3 mile from Hwy.
246 via 7th St.

**APPELLATIONS:** Paso Robles,
Russian River Valley, Santa
Lucia Highlands, Sonoma
Coast, Sta. Rita Hills.

**HOURS:** Noon–5 P.M.
Friday–Sunday.

**TASTINGS:** $10 for 8 wines.

**TOURS:** None.

**THE WINES:** Cabernet/
Mourvèdre, Chardonnay,
Grenache/Mourvèdre,
Pinot Noir.

**SPECIALTIES:** Vineyard-
designated Pinot Noir.

**WINEMAKERS:** Brian Loring
and Kimberly Loring.

**ANNUAL PRODUCTION:**
6,500 cases.

**OF SPECIAL NOTE:** AVA-
designated Pinot Noir
wines (Russian River Val-
ley, Santa Lucia Highlands,
and Sta. Rita Hills) available only in tasting room.

**NEARBY ATTRACTIONS:**
Historic Mission La
Purísima; Old Town Lom-
poc Heritage Walk (1-mile
scenic tour with 18 stops);
Jalama Beach County Park
(tidepooling, nature trails,
camping, surfing).

**B**rian Loring has pursued an obsession with Pinot Noir since the early 1980s, when he worked at a wine shop stocked with great Pinot Noir wines from France. At the time Loring was not impressed with American versions of the variety. But one day he literally tripped over a case of Pinot Noir from Calera Wine Company, tried it, and liked it very much. He contacted winemaker Josh Jensen, who proved to Loring that first-rate Pinot Noir could be made in California. He vowed to open his mind and palate to domestic possibilities in the coming years.

For more than a decade, Loring pursued his Pinot Noir interests in his free time. One day, while attending a wine show, he tasted Cottonwood Canyon's 1990 Santa Maria Pinot Noir. The quality so impressed him that every Cottonwood Canyon event Norm Beko. Beko invited Loring crush. Loring then decided to He began with 150 cases in 1999 2006, when he focused his full sister, Kimberly, began working 2004, they have been co-owners

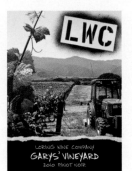

he spent several years attending and conversing with winemaker to learn firsthand during the 1997 launch the Loring Wine Company. and expanded to 6,000 cases by attention on his new career. His with the company in 2001. Since and co-winemakers.

Today the Lorings are con- sidered some of California's top Pinot Noir winemakers—their wines have made the *Wine Spectator* Top 100 list multiple years since 2004. Self-proclaimed nonfarmers, they are fanatical about sourcing grapes from trusted vineyards, including three in the nearby Sta. Rita Hills appellation. The Lorings give the vineyards free reign to farm their acres according to the same high standards in which they grow their own grapes. Brian and Kimberly, however, decide when to pick the grapes, which often hang longer on the vine than most, resulting in bigger, bolder flavor, their signature style. The company's labels showcase the importance of the vineyards—each has a black-and-white image of the particular fruit source. The Lorings' many sources enable them to produce a broad range of wines. Their 2010 vintages, for example, include thirteen different Pinot Noirs, four Chardonnays, and several blends. Since they have a particular aversion to cork taint, 100 percent of their bottles have had screwcaps since 2004.

This array of wines takes center stage at the tasting room in the Lompoc Wine Ghetto, an industrial park of blue-and-white metal buildings. The tasting bar is a simple row of barrels topped with a plank and a tablecloth. Numerous framed press accolades hang on the walls, testament to the Loring duo's prodigious talents. The minimalist setting enables visitors to focus on the results of their longtime passion for crafting wines from a special grape—the delicate Pinot Noir.

# PRESQU'ILE WINERY

For generations, the Murphy family traveled from their native Arkansas to the Mississippi Gulf Coast for holidays. The close-knit, multigenerational family eventually purchased eighteen acres in the area, built a family home, and named it Presqu'ile (French for "almost an island"). The moniker was inspired by the landscape: a narrow strip of land was the property's only connection to the mainland. Over the years, as various family members constructed additional homes, Presqu'ile grew into a multigenerational compound. In 2005 the entire estate was wiped out by Hurricane Katrina, and the Murphy family decided to embark on a new venture out west.

Matt Murphy cut his teeth in the wine business working in wineries in the Napa Valley and later at highly regarded Bien Nacido Vineyard in the Santa Maria Valley appellation of Santa Barbara County. He and his parents, Madison and Suzanne Murphy, searched for an ideal setting for a vineyard and winery. In 2007 they pur-  chased two hundred acres in Orcutt and established Presqu'ile Winery. They recognized the potential of the Santa Maria appellation, where cooling ocean breezes flow west to east between two mountain ranges, creating the ideal *terroir* for Pinot Noir and Chardonnay. Two generations form the core business: Madison and Suzanne; Matt and his wife, Amanda; Matt's brother, Jonathan, and his wife, Lindsay; and Matt and Jonathan's sister, Anna. Winemaker Dieter Cronje and vineyard manager Jim Stollberg complete the main operational team.

Presqu'ile planted seventy-three acres of sustainably farmed estate vineyards in 2008 and 2009: Pinot Noir and Chardonnay, the flagship varieties, along with Sauvignon Blanc and small lots of Syrah and Nebbiolo. A sustainable approach to building and farming has long been a priority for the Murphy family, whose Louisiana preservation efforts earned them the prestigious National Wetland Conservation Award in 2004. At their Orcutt estate, they have successfully preserved critical habitat for foxes, bobcats, owls, bats, and other natural predators while developing a major winery destination. Construction of a state-of-the-art winery, caves, and hospitality center is scheduled for completion in early 2013. The wines currently are produced in a temporary winery building.

In the meantime, visitors can enjoy Presqu'ile wines at a sophisticated, contemporary tasting room in Los Olivos. The lineup includes single-vineyard Pinot Noir, Chardonnay, and Sauvignon Blanc, in addition to Rosé and Syrah. The Presqu'ile wine label reflects a nautical theme—a nod to the Murphy family's long-held love of sailing, fishing, and other maritime activities at their beloved Gulf Coast home of "almost an island."

**PRESQU'ILE WINERY**
2369 Alamo Pintado Ave.
Los Olivos, CA 93441
805-688-2022
info@presquilewine.com
www.presquilewine.com

**OWNERS:** Murphy family.

**LOCATION:** Downtown Los Olivos, west of the flagpole.

**APPELLATION:** Santa Maria Valley.

**HOURS:** 11 A.M.–5 P.M. Wednesday–Sunday.

**TASTINGS:** $10 for 4 wines.

**TOURS:** None.

**THE WINES:** Chardonnay, Pinot Noir, Rosé, Sauvignon Blanc, Syrah.

**SPECIALTIES:** Estate and Santa Maria Valley Pinot Noir.

**WINEMAKER:** Dieter Cronje.

**ANNUAL PRODUCTION:** 2,100 cases.

**OF SPECIAL NOTE:** Rim Rock Pinot Noir available only in tasting room. Caves in north Santa Barbara County are scheduled for completion in early 2013.

**NEARBY ATTRACTIONS:** Wildling Art Museum (art of the American wilderness); historic buildings in Los Olivos and Ballard; Clairmont Farm Lavender Company; Quicksilver Miniature Horse Ranch.

# QUPÉ

O ne of Santa Barbara County's pioneering winemakers, Bob Lindquist worked his first harvest in 1975. Four years later, while laboring as a tour guide and cellar rat at Zaca Mesa Winery, he tasted a singular French Syrah that aroused an enduring devotion to Rhône-style wines. In 1982 Lindquist founded Qupé and proceeded to make the first Syrah and Viognier in Santa Barbara County, followed by California's earliest Marsanne.

Qupé (pronounced *kyoo-pay*) continues to specialize in Rhône-style wines, both blends and single-vineyard offerings that demonstrate the diverse flavor profiles of Santa Barbara County fruit. Grape sources include Santa Maria's historic Bien Nacido Vineyard, planted in the early 1970s. In 1986 Lindquist leased the fourteen-acre Ibarra-Young Vineyard and has farmed it or-ganically since 1999. He grafted the original Cabernet Sauvignon vines to Rhône varieties, and added four acres of Spanish Albariño, Tempranillo, and Graciano. Lindquist's wife and business partner, Louisa Sawyer-Lindquist, makes the Spanish varieties into wine under her label, Verdad. Sawyer-Lindquist, who had worked several harvests at a Long Island vineyard, discovered Spanish-style wines in the late 1990s. She met Lindquist in 1994 and, with his guidance, made her first wines, a 2000 Albariño and a 2001 Tempranillo.

In 2005 the Lindquists planted forty acres of grapes in the Edna Valley appellation, including Rhône and Spanish varieties, as well as Pinot Noir. In 2009 the vineyard was certified biodynamic by Demeter, a program that sets international standards for treating the land as a living agricultural system. The Lindquists make Qupé and Verdad at the facility they share with Au Bon Climat, founded by Jim Clendenen, an area winemaker and fellow vinicultural pioneer. Longtime friends, Lindquist and Clendenen built the winery in 1989, on land leased from Bien Nacido Vineyard. Over the years, the pair has mentored dozens of winemakers, including Gary Burk (Costa de Oro Winery), Frank Ostini (Hartley-Ostini Wines), and Lindquist's sons, Ethan and Luke.

After nearly thirty years in the wine business, Lindquist opened his first tasting room in 2008. Wines poured include Qupé, Verdad, and Ethan, his son's label. The tasting room is housed in a corner suite of a two-story building that resembles a Victorian-era home. Inside, a cherry tasting bar is topped with rosy-hued bubinga, a wood from central Africa. Hanging in the front window is a stained glass rendering of the Qupé logo, a stylized California poppy amid round buds and swirling stems. Lindquist chose the arresting image to illustrate the word *qupé*, "poppy" in Chumash, the language of Santa Barbara County's indigenous people.

**QUPÉ**
2963 Grand Ave.
Los Olivos, CA 93441
805-686-4200
tastingroom@qupe.com
www.qupe.com

**OWNERS:** Bob Lindquist, Louisa Sawyer-Lindquist.

**LOCATION:** .2 mile south of the intersection of Hwy. 154 and Grand Ave.

**APPELLATIONS:** Edna Valley, Santa Maria Valley, Santa Ynez Valley.

**HOURS:** 11 A.M.–5 P.M. daily.

**TASTINGS:** $10 for 8 wines. $20 for 6 reserve wines (noon, 2 P.M., and 3:30 P.M., Saturday and Sunday only). Wine-and-cheese pairing ($30) by appoint-ment.

**TOURS:** None.

**THE WINES:** Albariño, Chardonnay, Grenache, Marsanne, Roussanne, Syrah, Tempranillo, Viognier.

**SPECIALTIES:** Syrah, Rhône-style blends, Spanish-style wines.

**WINEMAKERS:** Bob Lindquist, Louisa-Sawyer Lindquist.

**ANNUAL PRODUCTION:** 40,000 cases.

**OF SPECIAL NOTE:** Quarterly themed events, listed on website, feature particular vineyards and grape va-rieties. Los Olivos Cuvée, Viognier, and single-vineyard Syrah available only in tasting room.

**NEARBY ATTRACTIONS:** Wild-ling Art Museum (art of the American wilderness); historic buildings in Los Olivos and Ballard; Clair-mont Lavender Company; Quicksilver Miniature Horse Ranch.

# TERCERO WINES

Los Olivos, a bucolic village in the heart of Santa Barbara County, has retained the Old West atmosphere that prevailed during its 1800s stagecoach days. A tall flagpole marks the center of town, and just a block away, the Tercero Wines tasting room occupies an intimate space in a Victorian-style building. When visitors open the door, they depart the historic Old California vibe and step into a friendly, contemporary world in which winemaker Larry Schaffer presents a fresh, unpretentious approach to wine tasting.

Schaffer entered the winemaking business relatively recently. He and his wife, Christie MacDonald, a physical therapist, had met as undergraduates at the University of California, Davis. Schaffer subsequently transferred to U.C. Berkeley and earned a bachelor's degree in business. He then worked as a sales and marketing executive in music and educational publishing for nearly two decades. He, his wife, and three young children were living in Orange County, California, when Schaffer decided to change careers. Winemaking intrigued him, as it would enable him to marry his sales and marketing background with his technical and scientific interests. He enrolled at U.C. Davis again, this time for a master's degree in viticulture and enology, and commuted every week.

In 2005 Schaffer landed a job as an enologist at Fess Parker Winery in Santa Barbara County and moved his family to Los Olivos. He started making his own wines in 2006. He and his wife named the new venture "tercero," Spanish for "third" (they have three children, and they met in the Tercero dormitory at U.C. Davis). In the summer of 2011, Schaffer left his position at Fess Parker Winery to devote full attention to his own business. He sources grapes from several local vineyards and crafts more than a dozen red and white Rhône varietal wines each year. He especially loves Grenache and offers three single-vineyard bottlings and several blends with the fruit.

Those who sample Schaffer's wines won't find tasting notes to accompany pours. Schaffer doesn't believe he should dictate to others how the wines should look, smell, and taste. Instead, he encourages visitors to write their own notes as they check out the day's flights listed on a chalkboard. Behind the stainless steel bar, the effervescent, loquacious Schaffer is often on hand to pour samples and to educate guests about winemaking. Describing himself as a "cheerleader" for Santa Barbara County wine country, he serves on the boards of the Santa Barbara County Vintners' Association and of the Rhone Rangers, a nonprofit organization of winemakers and growers devoted to promoting American Rhône-style wines. As visitors discover, he is always eager to share his knowledge and passion.

**TERCERO WINES**
2445 Alamo Pintado Ave., Ste. 104
Los Olivos, CA 93441
805-245-9584
larry@tercerowines.com
www.tercerowines.com

**OWNERS:** Larry Schaffer and Christie MacDonald.

**LOCATION:** Downtown Los Olivos; front door is on San Marcos Ave.

**APPELLATIONS:** Various within Santa Barbara County.

**HOURS:** Noon–5 or 6 P.M. Friday–Monday.

**TASTINGS:** $10 for 5 or 6 wines.

**TOURS:** None.

**THE WINES:** Gewürztraminer, Grenache, Grenache Blanc, Mourvèdre, Petite Sirah, Syrah, Viognier.

**SPECIALTIES:** Red and white Rhône wines.

**WINEMAKER:** Larry Schaffer.

**ANNUAL PRODUCTION:** 1,200 cases.

**OF SPECIAL NOTE:** Winemaker Larry Schaffer is often in the tasting room, pouring wine for guests. Many limited production, single-vineyard wines available only in tasting room.

**NEARBY ATTRACTIONS:** Wildling Art Museum (art of the American wilderness); historic buildings in Los Olivos and Ballard; Clairmont Farm Lavender Company; Quicksilver Miniature Horse Ranch.

# ZACA MESA WINERY & VINEYARDS

**ZACA MESA WINERY & VINEYARDS**
6905 Foxen Canyon Rd.
Los Olivos, CA 93441
805-688-9339
800-350-7972
info@zacamesa.com
www.zacamesa.com

**OWNERS:** John and Lou Cushman.

**LOCATION:** 9.4 miles north of Hwy. 154.

**APPELLATION:** Santa Ynez Valley.

**HOURS:** 10 A.M.–4 P.M. daily.

**TASTINGS:** $10 for 6 wines.

**TOURS:** None.

**THE WINES:** Chardonnay, Cinsault, Grenache, Mourvèdre, Roussanne, Syrah, Viognier, Z Blanc (Roussanne, Grenache Blanc, Viognier blend), Z Cuvée (Grenache, Mourvèdre, Syrah, Cinsault blend, depending on vintage), Z Gris (rosé), Z Three (Syrah, Grenache, Mourvèdre blend).

**SPECIALTY:** Estate-grown Syrah.

**WINEMAKER:** Eric Mohseni.

**ANNUAL PRODUCTION:** 35,000 cases.

**OF SPECIAL NOTE:** Grassy courtyard with picnic tables and life-size chessboard. Hiking trail rises to 1,500-foot elevation and spectacular views of Santa Ynez Valley.

**NEARBY ATTRACTION:** Historic 1875 San Ramon Chapel (Benjamin Foxen Memorial Chapel).

The Foxen Canyon Wine Trail snakes its way for twenty miles through some of California's most scenic countryside. At its highest point is a wild region, where deer, mountain lions, and even black bears still roam the hills. The native Chumash revered the site, calling it *zaca,* or "restful place."

In 1972 a group including real estate investor John Cushman purchased the 1,750-acre property, originally part of the 1830s Rancho La Zaca Mexican land grant. In 1973 they started the Zaca Mesa vineyard on soil that was once covered in prehistoric ocean dunes. Initial plantings included Cabernet Sauvignon, Chardonnay, Merlot, Zinfandel, Pinot Noir, and Riesling. The early fruit and vintages showed great promise, and in 1978 Zaca Mesa built a winery, which was expanded in 1981 into one of the region's first tasting rooms. In 1978 Zaca Mesa planted the first Syrah in Santa Barbara County, in a vineyard block that continues to provide low-yield grapes with intense flavor for the winery's coveted Black Bear Syrah. Many now-famous winemakers spent their early years at Zaca Mesa and later founded their own labels.

Few other vineyards existed in the region in the early 1970s. Zaca Mesa experimented with grape varieties for twenty years to determine which grew best in their microclimates and soils. This grape-growing experience determined Zaca Mesa's path from the 1990s onward: Rhône varieties prosper here, warmed by the sun early in the day and cooled by ocean breezes flowing through Los Alamos Valley to the vineyard from thirty miles away. The winery shifted its focus to Syrah and Rhône blends with great success. *Wine Spectator* placed the 1993 Zaca Mesa Syrah sixth on its Top 100 Wines list in 1995 and in 2010 ranked the 2006 Syrah at twenty-ninth.

Zaca Mesa now nurtures 240 acres of vineyards, follows sustainable growing practices, and keeps all fruit for its own estate wines. The visitor center, a lofty cedar structure designed to fit into the surroundings, looks much the same as it did nearly thirty years ago: cedar floors, soaring two-story ceilings, and gifts, cheeses, olives, and crackers displayed atop oak barrels. A U-shaped tasting bar with an aged zinc top and wood planks evokes the same rustic character as the original room. Outdoors, visitors are encouraged to sit in the grassy, oak-shaded courtyard, where they can play chess with knee-high pieces, picnic, and relax after hiking on the estate's scenic nature trail in ancient Chumash territory.

# SAN LUIS OBISPO COUNTY

San Luis Obispo County is divided into two distinct growing regions by the rugged Santa Lucia Range. Rising parallel to the coastline, the range separates the south, with its volcanic soils and mild, maritime climate, from the north, a region of fossil-studded soils and fifty-degree temperature swings. U.S. 101, extending north-south through the county, crosses the range at Cuesta Grade, where coastal plains meet the higher elevation oak woodlands. Along the coast, Highway 1 winds past the towns of Cambria, Morro Bay, and Pismo Beach. North at San Simeon, the magnificent Hearst Castle overlooks the Pacific Ocean.

In 1922 San Luis Obispo County's nascent wine industry garnered international attention when Polish pianist Ignace Paderewski planted Zinfandel vines near Paso Robles. When the 1960s brought success with Pinot Noir in vineyards on the west side of Paso Robles, wine grapes began to replace cattle ranches and hot springs as the county's dominant features. The 1973 planting of Paragon Vineyard established Edna Valley, near the city of San Luis Obispo, as a prime grape-growing area. Since the early 1980s, vinicultural growth has exploded, especially in the region north of Cuesta Grade, which is home to 75 percent of San Luis Obispo County's two-hundred-plus wineries.

In response to industry expansion, local viticulturists formed the Central Coast Vineyard Team to promote sustainable farming. The group developed a program called Sustainability in Practice (SIP), featuring a rigorous set of standards in areas ranging from environmental stewardship to labor relations. Wineries and vineyards meeting these standards earn SIP certification, which verifies their efforts to protect workers, the environment, and business stability. To date, fifty California wineries, 27,000 vineyard acres, and 300,000 cases of wine have been SIP certified.

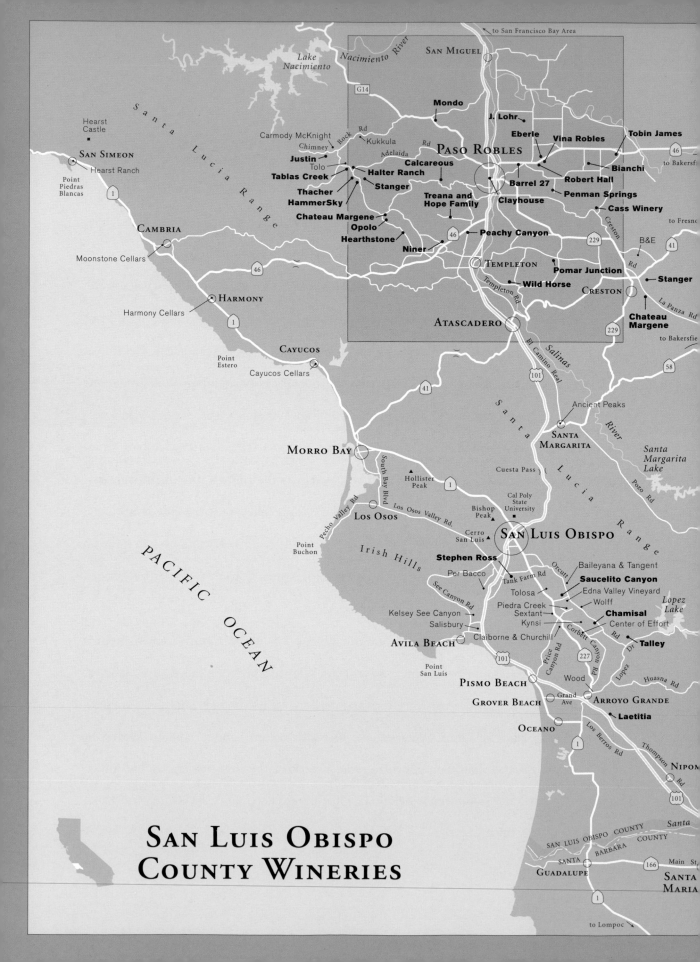

# SAN LUIS OBISPO COUNTY WINERIES

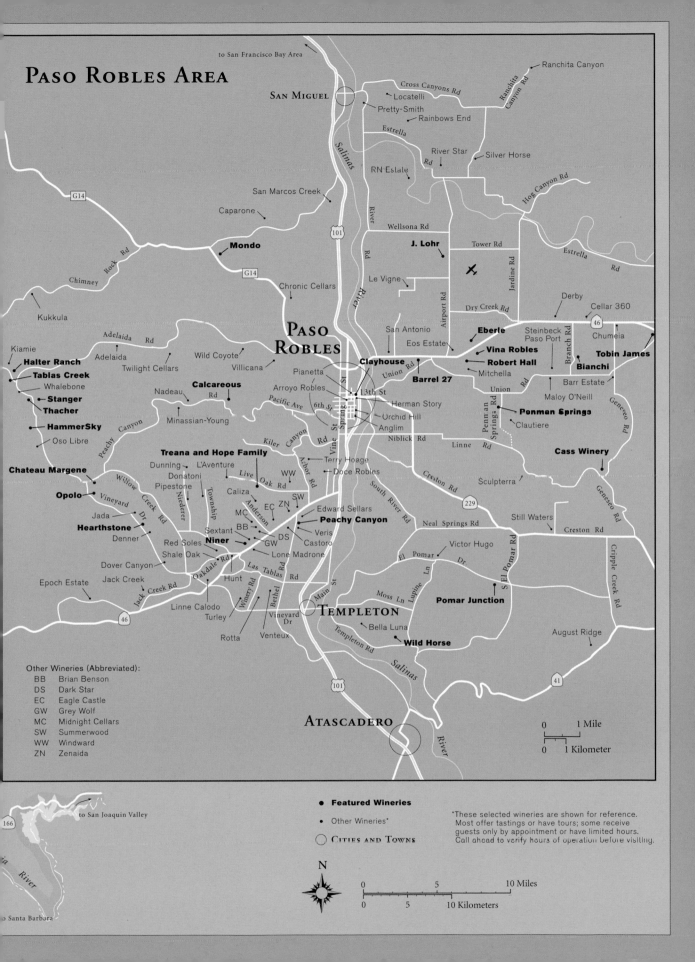

# PASO ROBLES AREA

to San Francisco Bay Area

SAN MIGUEL

Cross Canyons Rd

Ranchita Canyon

Locatelli
Pretty-Smith
Rainbows End

Ranchita Canyon Rd

Estrella

River Star Rd

Silver Horse

Hog Canyon Rd

RN Estate

Estrella Rd

G14

San Marcos Creek

Wellsona Rd

Caparone

Tower Rd

Mondo

J. Lohr

G14

Le Vigne

Derby

Chronic Cellars

Dry Creek Rd

Cellar 360

46

Chimney Rock Rd

PASO ROBLES

San Antonio

Eberle

Steinbeck Paso Port

Chumeia

Kukkula

Eos Estate

Vina Robles

Branch Rd

Tobin James

Kiamie

Adelaida Rd

Clayhouse

Robert Hall

Bianchi

Halter Ranch

Adelaida

Wild Coyote

Pianetta

Union Rd

Mitchella

Barr Estate

Tablas Creek

Villicana

Arroyo Robles

Barrel 27

Union Rd

Maloy O'Neill

Whalebone

Calcareous

13th St

Herman Story

Penman Springs

Geneseo Rd

Nadeau

Pacific Ave

6th St

Urchid Hill

Clautiere

Stanger

Rd

Anglim

Thacher

Minassian-Young

Kiler Canyon Rd

Niblick Rd

Linne Rd

Cass Winery

HammerSky

Oso Libre

Peachy Canyon Rd

Treana and Hope Family

Live Oak Rd

WW

Terry Hoage

Creston Rd

Sculpterra

Chateau Margene

Dunning

L'Aventure

ZN

Doce Robles

Donatoni

SW

Niederer

EC

Opolo

Pipestone

Caliza

Township

Anderson

Edward Sellars

Jada

Vineyard Dr

MC

Neal Springs Rd

Still Waters

229

Hearthstone

BB

Peachy Canyon

Victor Hugo

Creston Rd

Denner

Sextant

DS

Veris

Red Soles

Niner

GW

Castoro

El Pomar Dr

Shale Oak

Lone Madrone

Geneseo Rd

Dover Canyon

Jack Creek

Hunt

Las Tablas Rd

Moss Ln

Lupine Ln

Pomar Junction

Cripple Creek Rd

Epoch Estate

Jack Creek Rd

Oakdale Rd

Bethel Rd

Templeton

August Ridge

46

Linne Calodo

Winery Rd

Turley

Vineyard Dr

Bella Luna

Rotta

Venteux

Wild Horse

41

Templeton Rd

Salinas

South River Rd

Main St

101

ATASCADERO

River

## Other Wineries (Abbreviated):

| | |
|---|---|
| BB | Brian Benson |
| DS | Dark Star |
| EC | Eagle Castle |
| GW | Grey Wolf |
| MC | Midnight Cellars |
| SW | Summerwood |
| WW | Windward |
| ZN | Zenaida |

0       1 Mile

0       1 Kilometer

166

to San Joaquin Valley

• **Featured Wineries**

• Other Wineries*

◯ **CITIES AND TOWNS**

*These selected wineries are shown for reference. Most offer tastings or have tours; some receive guests only by appointment or have limited hours. Call ahead to verify hours of operation before visiting.

River

to Santa Barbara

N

0          5          10 Miles

0          5          10 Kilometers

Salinas River

# BARREL 27 WINE COMPANY

A spirited operation with blue-collar beginnings, Barrel 27 Wine Company specializes in Rhône-style wines. Co-founder and winemaker McPrice Myers prefers the winemaking style of Châteauneuf-du-Pape and strives to craft vintages that reflect similar old-world complexities. Myers discovered his vinicultural calling in the mid-1990s while managing a Trader Joe's, in Orange County, California. After tasting through the store's eclectic inventory of wines, he resolved to learn more about winemaking. Myers began traveling to the wineries of Santa Barbara and San Luis Obispo counties, and he even volunteered to work as a cellar rat at a number of respected Central Coast producers.

While on the Central Coast, Myers became friends with Russell From, a local resident and fellow aspiring winemaker. Determined to start small, the pair founded the winery in 2002. At the time, both were twenty-seven years old, a number they deemed ideal for the company's name. The partners purchased fruit from local growers and made Rhône-style wine at Central Coast Wine Services, in Santa Maria. They sold the finished product strictly through wholesale channels. One of those channels was a Southern California wine store managed by Jason Carter, whose enthusiasm for the product spilled over into his sales pitches. Carter sold nearly all of the company's first vintage, which numbered 150 cases. Myers and From, who left the business in 2011, doubled production each of the following two years. When their annual production reached 500 cases, they brought in Carter as co-owner and general manager of the burgeoning company.

By 2009, fans of the wine were clamoring for a place to visit the winemakers and taste their portfolio. The company moved to an industrial space in Paso Robles, where it is currently located, although a move to a larger facility is planned in the near future. The tasting room has housed some of the region's most distinguished wineries. In the early 1990s, Matt Garretson opened Garretson Wine Company in the then new building. Other renowned tenants have included Saxum Vineyards, Linne Calodo Winery, and Villa Creek Cellars. The copper-topped bar that Garretson installed parallels the back wall of the simple space. Wooden sheathing made of the printed sides of French wine grape boxes covers the front of the bar. Behind the bar, windows offer a peek into the winery, where Myers crafts small-lot reserve wines. The rest of the wines are made at Paso Robles Wine Services. The wines bear fanciful names, such as High on the Hog, referring to wild pigs roaming the source vineyard, and Hand Over Fist, an ever-changing Rhône-style blend.

**BARREL 27 WINE COMPANY**
2323 Tuley Ct., Ste. 110
Paso Robles, CA 93446
805-237-1245
info@barrel27.com
www.barrel27.com

**OWNERS:** McPrice Myers, Jason Carter, David Graves.

**LOCATION:** .5 mile southeast of the intersection of Hwy. 46 East and Golden Hill Rd. (Call ahead to confirm location.)

**APPELLATION:** Paso Robles.

**HOURS:** 11 A.M.–5 P.M. daily.

**TASTINGS:** $10 for 7 wines (applicable to purchase).

**TOURS:** By appointment.

**THE WINES:** Cabernet Sauvignon, Grenache Blanc, Grenache Noir, Moscato, Mourvèdre, Roussanne, Syrah, Tempranillo, Viognier, Zinfandel.

**SPECIALTY:** Rhône-style wines.

**WINEMAKER:** McPrice Myers.

**ANNUAL PRODUCTION:** 12,000 cases.

**OF SPECIAL NOTE:** Tasting room offers wine-of-the-month special sales, and olive oil and vinegar samples.

**NEARBY ATTRACTIONS:** Downtown Paso Robles; Paso Robles City Park (site of festivals, summer concerts, farmers' market); Barney Schwartz Park (lake, picnic areas).

# BIANCHI WINERY & TASTING ROOM

**BIANCHI WINERY &
TASTING ROOM**
3380 Branch Rd.
Paso Robles, CA 93446
805-226-9922
info@bianchiwine.com
www.bianchiwine.com

**OWNERS:** Glenn Bianchi,
Beau Bianchi.

**LOCATION:** 6 miles east of
downtown Paso Robles.

**APPELLATION:** Paso Robles.

**HOURS:** 10 A.M.–5 P.M. daily.

**TASTINGS:** $5 for 7 wines.
Reservations recommended
for groups of 10 or more.

**TOURS:** By appointment.

**THE WINES:** Barbera,
Cabernet Franc, Cabernet
Sauvignon, Chardonnay,
Merlot, Moscato, Petite
Sirah, Pinot Grigio, Pinot
Noir, Refosco, Sangiovese,
Sauvignon Blanc, Syrah,
Zinfandel, several blends.

**SPECIALTIES:** Cabernet
Sauvignon, Merlot, Petite
Sirah, Syrah, Zen Ranch
Zinfandel.

**WINEMAKER:** Tom Lane.

**ANNUAL PRODUCTION:**
20,000 cases.

**OF SPECIAL NOTE:** Deli foods
sold in tasting room. Gift
shop with clothing, pottery,
and wine accessories. Vineyard House, a renovated
farmhouse, offers overnight
lodging. Wines including
Barbera, Cabernet Franc,
Moscato, Refosco, and
Sangiovese available only in
tasting room.

**NEARBY ATTRACTIONS:**
Barney Schwartz Park
(lake, picnic areas);
Estrella Warbird Museum
(restored military aircraft,
memorabilia).

The rural road that leads to the Bianchi estate in the bucolic Paso Robles countryside traverses a series of oak-studded rolling hills, blanketed by vineyards, row crops, and pastures. Suddenly, as visitors drive through the estate entrance, an oasis rises amid the undulating knolls: a waterfall-fed lake and a striking complex of modern structures. Migrating birds skim across the water next to a lakeside deck, stone terraces, and a dramatic visitor center—a contemporary interpretation of an old California mission in adobe, wood, and stone. A stunning green-toned winery facility with a corrugated tin roof sits on a gentle rise a short walk from the visitor center. This serene, water-oriented scene reflects owner Glenn Bianchi's desire to create not just a winery and hospitality center, but an attractive destination where travelers can take a break and enjoy the natural setting.

The Bianchi family's involvement in the wine industry dates to 1974, when Glenn and his father, Joseph, invested in a winery and vineyard on the banks of the San Joaquin River in the Central Valley. The business grew into a large-scale producer of wines for the general consumer. In the late 1990s, Glenn actively pursued a longtime dream of finding a place where he could grow and source premium grapes to make world-class wines. After a statewide search for a vineyard site, he settled on Paso Robles, impressed by the caliber of the regional wines and by the pristine natural landscapes. In January 2000, Bianchi purchased a forty-acre property on the east side of Paso Robles. Sparing no expense, he soon began construction of the visitor center and a state-of-the-art winery with computer-controlled fermentation tanks, and developed a small pond into a scenic lake. In the twenty-acre vineyard, he replanted the existing Cabernet vines and added Syrah, Merlot, and Zinfandel varieties. Winemaker Tom Lane, who has more than two decades of winemaking experience, joined Bianchi as director of winemaking in 2005. He crafts ultrapremium wines from estate fruit and selects high-quality grapes (mostly Italian varieties) from other Central Coast growers to create an array of small-lot wines.

The visitor center blends modern design elements with traditional materials. Glass walls soar up toward cathedral ceilings with metal beams, stainless steel and glass accents adorn the maple tasting bar and display cabinets, and a stone fireplace fronts a comfortable lounge area with dark red leather and cherrywood furniture. The center extends outdoors to a spacious deck overlooking the lake and vineyards, where guests are invited to enjoy Bianchi wines, observe the wildlife, and relax to the soothing sounds of the waterfall and the cooling breezes from the lake.

# CALCAREOUS VINEYARD

The owners and staff at Calcareous Vineyard invite visitors to come for the wine and stay for the sense of place, a compelling offer of liquid art and authentic landscape. Named after the chalky soil that distinguishes its west side *terroir,* the hilltop winery features a thick lawn dotted with tables and chairs, an official bocce ball court, and a stunning panorama of hills, oaks, and sky. With glass walls made of accordion doors that can be collapsed to admit air and even more light, the tasting room serves as a fitting showcase for both the lush wines and the site's considerable attributes.

Inside, stone pillars contrast with the mahogany hues of the open-beamed ceiling and tasting bar, and the open floor space allows plenty of room for mingling with other tasters, browsing the display tables, or catching the endless view. The tasting room opened in 2008, after a smaller one in the winery proved to be too limited, and was named Lloyd's Lookout, in honor of Lloyd Messer, the winery's visionary cofounder. Messer was a traveling man whose Iowa-based beer and wine distributing business frequently brought him

to Paso Robles, where he enjoyed rubbing elbows with area winemakers and dreaming about a different kind of life. When he sold his business to become a grape grower in the late 1990s, he asked his daughter, Dana Brown, to join him as a partner. Brown, who had started a wine distributorship after college, was ready for a career change after having her first child. She caught her dad's enthusiasm, sold her business, and headed west.

In 2000 the pair purchased nearly eight hundred acres of land, but not before securing fruit for the winery's 1999 debut vintage of Chardonnay and Pinot Noir. Eager and impatient, they planted a twenty-five-acre vineyard and continued to make wine at neighboring facilities with purchased fruit, until opening their own winery in March 2006. When their vineyard began producing, they dedicated the Calcareous label to their estate program, and Twisted Sisters, a label wryly named for Brown and her younger sister, Erika Messer, to wines made from nonestate fruit.

Since Lloyd's unexpected death in May 2006, Brown and Messer have shouldered the details of the business. The sisters continue to build the brand and celebrate his daring dream. Atop a chunk of calcareous soil in a flowerbed beside the tasting room, they have placed a bronzed pair of Lloyd's old work boots, a loving tribute to the man whose vision started it all.

**CALCAREOUS VINEYARD**
3430 Peachy Canyon Rd.
Paso Robles, CA 93446
805-239-0289
info@calcareous.com
www.calcareous.com

**OWNERS:** Dana Brown, Erika Messer.

**LOCATION:** 3 miles west of downtown Paso Robles.

**APPELLATION:** Paso Robles.

**HOURS:** 11 A.M.–5 P.M. daily.

**TASTINGS:** $10 for 6–8 wines.

**TOURS:** By appointment.

**THE WINES:** Bordeaux blend, Cabernet Sauvignon, Chardonnay, Petit Verdot, Pinot Noir, Rhône blend, Roussanne, Syrah, Viognier, Zinfandel.

**SPECIALTIES:** Tres Violet (Mourvèdre, Syrah, Grenache blend), Meritage.

**WINEMAKER:** Jason Joyce.

**ANNUAL PRODUCTION:** 10,500 cases.

**OF SPECIAL NOTE:** Picnic area with tables; bocce ball court. Food-and-wine pairing available weekends, noon–3 P.M. Gift shop stocks books, wine accessories, and light snacks.

**NEARBY ATTRACTION:** Paso Robles City Park (site of festivals, summer concerts, farmers' market).

# CASS WINERY

**CASS WINERY**
7350 Linne Rd.
Paso Robles, CA 93446
805-239-1730
info@casswines.com
www.casswines.com

**OWNERS:** Steve Cass,
Ted Plemons.

**LOCATION:** 7.2 miles east
of U.S. 101.

**APPELLATION:** Paso Robles.

**HOURS:** 11 A.M.–5 P.M. daily.

**TASTINGS:** $10 for 7 wines.

**TOURS:** On request.

**THE WINES:** Cabernet
Sauvignon, Grenache,
Marsanne, Mourvèdre,
Petite Sirah, Roussanne,
Syrah, Viognier.

**SPECIALTY:** Rockin' One
(Syrah, Mourvèdre, Petite
Sirah, Grenache blend).

**WINEMAKER:** Lood Kotze.

**ANNUAL PRODUCTION:**
5,000 cases.

**OF SPECIAL NOTE:** Wines are
100 percent estate grown.
On-site café serves gourmet
lunch daily 11 A.M.–5 P.M.
or by reservation. Annual
grape stomp and piano
concert held in the fall.

**NEARBY ATTRACTIONS:**
Barney Schwartz Park
(lake, picnic areas);
Estrella Warbird Museum
(restored military aircraft,
memorabilia).

Located at a country crossroads way off the beaten path, Cass Winery emerges like a lush mirage from among the alluvial hills east of Paso Robles. Bracketed by a 146-acre vineyard is a cream-colored winery and tasting room. Splashes of outdoor art, including a vintage railroad bell, old basket press, and flying angel weathervane, dot the grounds. Spreading oaks shade a rustic seating area. In front of the tasting room, tables and chairs make for a quiet retreat or picnic spot under a vine-entwined shelter.

Inside, visitors taste an array of estate wines, predominantly red Rhônes, poured on most days by Bryan Cass, son of Steve Cass, one of the winery's founding partners. Near the eye-catching silver tasting bar built of glass doors framed by the view into the barrel room. in front of an impromptu and in a softly lit space complete with commercial chef, serves a gourmet the appealing café menu

industrial diamond plate, rim of a giant cask afford a Colorful paintings hang collage crafted from corks, opposite, an informal café, kitchen and executive lunch daily. Specialties on include truffle pizza, crab cakes, and Cuban pork sandwiches, inviting fare for hungry travelers exploring what neighborhood producers call the Backroads Wineries.

Steve Cass and his business partner, Ted Plemons, who owns a local construction company, opened the winery in 2005 after falling under the spell of Rhône wines while on a trip to South Africa. They decided that they could grow comparable fruit in Paso Robles and were among the first growers in the United States to buy grapevines through ENTAV (Establissement National Technique pour l'Amélioration de la Viticulture), a French agency that field-tests plant material for health and vinicultural suitability. Cass credits the certified vines with his vineyard's uniform ripening, consistent quality, and immediate success.

Cass and Plemons hired South African winemaker Lood Kotze to craft wines similar to the ones they encountered on their trip. Under Kotze's skilled supervision, the wines have borne out their hunch about the region's potential to produce superior Rhônes and proven to be a mighty draw for wine lovers. Most arrive by car or bicycle to taste the wines and tuck into lunch, but more than one local has turned into the winery on horseback, making the stop while on a leisurely ride. The partners continue to sell 80 percent of their grapes to other California wineries, and they are delighted to have a cellar full of their favorite Rhône-style wines, grown and bottled in Paso Robles.

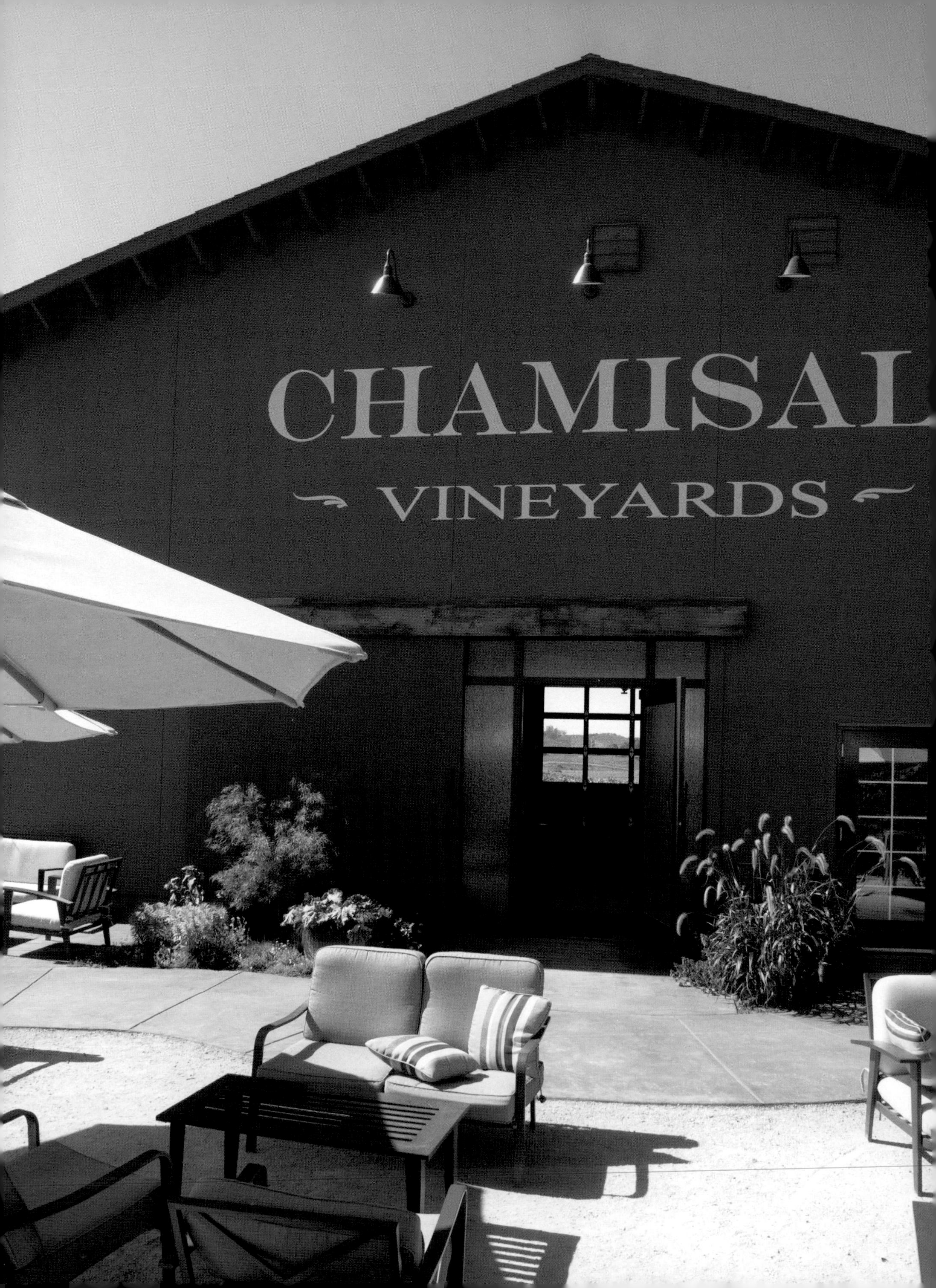
CHAMISAL
VINEYARDS

# CHAMISAL VINEYARDS

From February through March, dense stands of chamise, a native evergreen shrub with fragrant white flowers, cover more than seven million acres of California's hills with a magnificent blanket of "snow." These brushlands, also called *chamissal*, thrive in calcareous, clay-rich, nutrient-poor soil on dry, rocky slopes—the same challenging topography that encourages Pinot Noir and Chardonnay vines to produce flavorful grapes.

In 1973 the Goss family planted Chamisal Vineyards, the first vineyard in the Edna Valley appellation, in the chamise-speckled Santa Lucia Mountain foothills. In 1994 new owners purchased the property and renamed it the ideal conditions for growing nay, including the cool marine and planted a range of clones— stocks known to thrive in these longer on the vine and thereby Crimson Wine Group acquired the original name, Chamisal, to

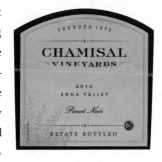

Domaine Alfred. They recognized quality Pinot Noir and Chardonnair flowing through the valley, genetically exact copies of root-conditions—whose fruit hangs develops rich, complex flavors. the estate in 2008 and restored honor the vineyard's history.

Today Chamisal Vineyards cultivates eighty-five acres planted with twenty-five different clones of five varietals, mostly Pinot Noir and Chardonnay. Each clonal selection matches a particular microclimate on the estate and expresses a subtle difference in flavor. All fieldwork is done by hand, and the estate's environmentally friendly farming methods incorporate organic and biodynamic principles. Winemaker Fintan du Fresne strives to make wines that reflect the vineyard's complex character—a blend of sweet and savory he calls "Chamisal Spice." He grew up in New Zealand, where his father, a well-known wine journalist, exposed him to the enology world, and where he studied ways in which geology affects *terroir*. He especially appreciates the estate's unusually broad range of clonal varieties, which give him many different options for creative blends.

Chamisal wines are poured in the rustic-chic tasting room in the original winery from the 1970s—a lofty barn, perched on a knoll amid the vineyards. Outdoors, a patio and picnic area provide alternative spaces for tasting and picnics. Long redwood tables, custom-made by a local artisan, encourage visitors to enjoy the pastoral vineyard and mountain views.

**CHAMISAL VINEYARDS**
7525 Orcutt Rd.
San Luis Obispo, CA 93401
805-541-9463
866-808-9463
tastingroom@chamisal
vineyards.com
www.chamisalvineyards.
com

**OWNER:** Crimson Wine Group.

**LOCATION:** 9 miles south of downtown San Luis Obispo and 2 miles south of Biddle Ranch Rd.

**APPELLATION:** Edna Valley

**HOURS:** 10 A.M.–5 P.M. daily.

**TASTINGS:** $10 for 5 or 6 wines. $15 for 5 or 6 reserve wines.

**TOURS:** None.

**THE WINES:** Chardonnay, Grenache, Pinot Gris, Pinot Noir, Syrah.

**SPECIALTIES:** Estate and Califa Selection Edna Valley Chardonnay and Pinot Noir, plus small-lot, cool-climate Grenache and Syrah.

**WINEMAKER:** Fintan du Fresne.

**ANNUAL PRODUCTION:** 20,000 cases.

**OF SPECIAL NOTE:** Pet-friendly outdoor picnic area. Special events include San Luis Obispo Vintner's Celebration (third weekend in June); vineyard concert (mid-July); Lobsterfest (first weekend in August); Harvest Celebration (first weekend in November). Pinot Gris, Grenache, Syrah, and reserve and select Pinot Noir available only in tasting room.

**NEARBY ATTRACTIONS:** Mission San Luis Obispo de Tolosa; San Luis Obispo County Historical Museum and other historic buildings in downtown San Luis Obispo; Pismo State Beach.

# CHATEAU MARGENE

**Chateau Margene**
4385 La Panza Rd.
Creston, CA 93432
805-238-2321

**Chateau Margene at Limerock Orchards**
6996 Peachy Canyon Rd.
Paso Robles, CA 93446
805-238-3500
info@chateaumargene.com
www.chateaumargene.com

**Owners:** Michael and Margene Mooney.

**Location:** Chateau Margene: 15 miles east of Paso Robles and Atascadero, 2.2 miles east of Hwy. 41. Chateau Margene at Limerock Orchards: 5.2 miles north of Hwy. 46 West.

**Appellation:** Paso Robles.

**Hours:** Chateau Margene: 11 A.M.–5 P.M. Saturday and Sunday. Chateau Margene at Limerock Orchards: 11 A.M.–5 P.M. daily.

**Tastings:** $10 for 5 wines (applicable to purchase).

**Tours:** With Barrel Room Experience, by appointment (805-238-2321).

**The Wines:** Cabernet Sauvignon, Grenache, Grenache Blanc, Mourvèdre, Petite Sirah, Pinot Noir.

**Specialties:** Bordeaux-style blends, Pinot Noir from the Santa Lucia Highlands.

**Winemaker:** Michael Mooney.

**Annual Production:** 3,000 cases.

**Of Special Note:** Picnic areas at both locations. All wines are available in tasting room only.

**Nearby Attractions:** East side: Town of Creston (country store, Friday night barbecue, September rodeo); Olivas de Oro Olive Company (100-year-old olive trees, olive oil tasting). West side: Farmstand 46 (deli, organic gardens).

A seventh-generation Californian, Mike Mooney and his wife, Margene, spent eight years searching for vineyard property on the West Coast before discovering the Paso Robles appellation. Amid the region's oak-studded hills, they recognized a distinctive *terroir* marked by lean soil, deep water, dazzling summer sun, and cool ocean breezes that moderate afternoon heat. The conditions promised to be ideal for ripening the Bordeaux-type grapes they wanted to grow. The couple planned to make the wine themselves and focus on quality by keeping their operation small.

In 1998 the Mooneys purchased twenty-two acres near Creston, on the extreme southeast side of the Paso Robles appellation. They property, which is located just thirty elevation of 1,200 feet. The couple vignon, Cabernet Franc, and Merlot came with the property and served the Mooneys were crafting their by 2001 they had built a modest

founded Chateau Margene on the miles from the ocean and at an planted six acres of Cabernet Sauvignon near the rambling farmhouse that as their new home. Within a year, own style of rich, bold wines, and winery near their estate vineyard.

Glass doors at one end of the winery open onto a shady, sofa-lined deck overlooking an expanse of green lawn. A path winds through a garden stocked with a variety of roses, and a small demonstration vineyard features Malbec and Petit Verdot vines. Inside the winery, the Mooneys turned a portion of the cellar into a tasting room. Racks of wine-filled barrels frame the tasting area, which is open on weekends and by appointment for what the Mooneys call the Barrel Room Experience. This unusual offering includes a tour of the winery with the winemaker himself, as well as an off-the-list tasting of special wines and barrel samples. In the cool half-light of the cellar, visitors enjoy an intimate look at the craft of winemaking and learn firsthand the changes that wines undergo during barrel aging.

In 2010 the Mooneys opened a second tasting room on the west side of Paso Robles. With its stone chimney, bay window, and wide covered porches, the tasting room resembles a modern country house. Opposite a side porch set with wicker seating, a lawn borders a sparkling pond. French doors open into the tasting room, which has two walnut-stained tasting bars topped with black granite. Here, staff members pour wines bottled under both the Chateau Margene and Mooney Family labels. Introduced in 2006, the Mooney Family label pays homage to the family business, which includes the Mooneys' two sons, Chris and Jon. The label showcases Rhône-style blends made from fruit grown in Paso Robles, as well as Pinot Noir from the cool Santa Lucia Highlands of Monterey County.

# CLAYHOUSE WINES

Located in the historic Grangers Union building in the heart of Paso Robles, Clayhouse Wines offers a comfortable spot for sipping wine and observing the downtown bustle. Visitors can relax in a window seat with a sidewalk view, or lounge in black leather chairs beside the fireplace at the back of the softly lit tasting room, opened in 2008. The open-beam ceiling, wall plaster reminiscent of an old adobe finish, and exposed bricks revealing the building's 1893-era construction lend an aura of antiquity to the otherwise modern room. A flat-panel monitor plays recorded scenes from the winery's vineyard, providing visual context and a glimpse of the wines' origins. Especially impressive are images of the stout,  forty-year-old vines that yield the label's signature Petite Sirah.

The 1,400-acre vineyard is located seventeen miles east of Paso Robles, off Highway 46 East. A land mark water fountain resembling giant grape clusters dropping a cascade of juice marks the entrance to the private property. The vine-yard supports twenty different wine grape varieties, as well as 400 acres of table grapes. The winery vinifies about 10 percent of the wine grapes and sells the remainder to wine-makers both regionally and statewide.

Detailed records of the vineyard property begin in the early 1860s when the Clarke family purchased it with Civil War scrip. Around 1863, the Clarkes fashioned bricks from local mud and built an adobe house that still stands near the driveway. They ran cattle on the land until they sold it in 1966. Wine grapes were planted in 1972, and twenty-one years later, the property was acquired by the Middleton family, whose members have owned a timber company in Washington state since 1898. When they ceased cutting trees in 1991, the Middletons diversified by buying table grape vineyards in California's Central Valley. To extend the growing season, they acquired the Paso Robles property, dubbed it Red Cedar Vineyard to acknowledge the trees they once harvested, and grafted over most of the vines to varieties better suited to the climate.

Vineyard practices include the use of falcons to discourage grape-devouring birds and owl boxes to house predators for rodent control. In 2011 Clayhouse Wines received the Sustainable Winegrow-ing Program certification from the California Sustainable Winegrowing Alliance in recognition of its environmental stewardship and adoption of sustainable techniques. Before launching the winery in 2003, CEO Rick Middleton learned all aspects of the wine business by working at Tom Eddy Winery in Napa Valley. When naming their new enterprise, he and his family chose Clayhouse, to honor the sturdy adobe home built so long ago.

**CLAYHOUSE WINES**
849 13th St.
Paso Robles, CA 93446
805-238-7055
info@clayhousewines.com
www.clayhousewines.com

**CEO:** Rick Middleton, Middleton Family Wines.

**LOCATION:** Downtown Paso Robles at the corner of 13th and Pine streets.

**APPELLATION:** Paso Robles.

**HOURS:** 11 A.M.–6 P.M. Sunday–Thursday, noon 7 P.M. Friday–Saturday.

**TASTINGS:** $5 for 5 wines (applicable to purchase).

**TOURS:** Of the vineyard and old adobe, by appointment ($40). Includes wine tasting.

**THE WINES:** Cabernet Sauvignon, Grenache Blanc, Malbec, Petite Sirah, Sauvignon Blanc, Syrah, Tannat, Tempranillo, Viognier, Zinfandel.

**SPECIALTIES:** Estate old-vine Petite Sirah, estate Adobe Red (Zinfandel-based blend).

**WINEMAKER:** Blake Kuhn.

**ANNUAL PRODUCTION:** 45,000 cases.

**OF SPECIAL NOTE:** Tasting room is child and pet friendly. Live music on Friday evenings during spring and summer. Extended hours and art displays the first Saturday of every month. Wines available by the glass. Many wines available in tasting room only.

**NEARBY ATTRACTIONS:** Paso Robles City Park (site of festivals, summer concerts, farmers' market); Paso Robles Pioneer Museum (historical displays, vintage vehicles and tractors).

# EBERLE WINERY

**EBERLE WINERY**
3810 Hwy. 46 East
Paso Robles, CA 93446
805-238-9607
tastingroom@eberlewinery.com
www.eberlewinery.com

**OWNERS/GENERAL PARTNERS:**
Gary and Marcy Eberle.

**LOCATION:** 3.5 miles east of
U.S. 101.

**APPELLATION:** Paso Robles.

**HOURS:** 10 A.M.–5 P.M. daily
in winter; 10 A.M.–6 P.M.
daily in summer.

**TASTINGS:** Complimentary
for 5 wines.

**TOURS:** Free guided cave
tours every half hour daily.
VIP tours ($25) include
reserve tasting; reservations
required.

**THE WINES:** Barbera, Caber-
net Sauvignon, Chardonnay,
Muscat Canelli, Sangiovese,
Syrah, Viognier, Zinfandel.

**SPECIALTIES:** Vineyard-
designated Cabernet
Sauvignon and Syrah,
vintage Port.

**WINEMAKER:** Ben Mayo.

**ANNUAL PRODUCTION:**
30,000 cases.

**OF SPECIAL NOTE:** Extensive
wine caves available for
touring. Monthly guest chef
dinners in caves. Picnic
deck overlooking vineyard;
on-site bocce ball court. Gift
shop offering ceramic ware,
wine and food books, gourmet foods, and clothing.
One-third of the winery's
production, including
library reserve wines, available only in tasting room.

**NEARBY ATTRACTIONS:**
Paso Robles City Park
(site of festivals, summer
concerts, farmers' market);
Estrella Warbird Museum
(restored military aircraft,
memorabilia).

I n Paso Robles, the name Eberle conjures two iconic figures: pioneering winemaker Gary Eberle, who planted the region's first Syrah vines and helped establish Paso Robles as a premier wine-growing region, and the small statue of a wild boar, the mascot of Eberle Winery. *Eberle* means "small boar" in German, and images of wild boars appear on the winery logo. A bronze boar, cast by Baroque master Pietro Tacca in 1620, sits at the winery entrance. *Il Porcellino*, a replica of the marble boar that once stood in the Uffizi in Florence, invites visitors to rub its snout and toss coins in the fountain beneath its feet—a Florentine tradition said to bring good luck.

This good fortune is most readily apparent at the expansive oak tasting bar, where samples of Eberle wines are poured at no charge, a rarity in the region. It also comes in the form of free guided tours through the 1,600 square feet of caves beneath the visitor center. The complimentary tours and tast-ings reflect Gary Eberle's firm belief in educating visitors about all aspects of winemaking so they form a personal connection to the bottles of wine they enjoy at the table.

Eberle's passion for wine, Cabernet Sauvignon in particular, developed when he was a doctoral student in cellular genetics at Louisiana State University. He decided he would rather be a winemaker and transferred to the enology doctoral program at U.C. Davis. In the early 1970s, he and his profes-sors made a few pilgrimages to Paso Robles to collect soil samples, and their research pinpointed Paso Robles as an area of great grape-growing promise. He moved there to cofound Estrella River Winery (now Meridian) and worked as head winemaker for nearly a decade. He planted Syrah vines in 1974—the first in the United States since the repeal of Prohibition—and was the first Paso Robles winemaker to make a 100 percent Syrah wine. Eberle officially established his own label and winery partnership in 1982, purchasing sixty-five acres just a few miles west of Estrella River Winery. That year he released his flagship wine, the 1979 Cabernet Sauvignon. He also helped establish the Paso Robles appellation and completed a utilitarian cedar winery building.

The Eberle estate vineyard now produces Cabernet, Chardonnay, and Muscat Canelli grapes exclusively for Eberle wines. Eberle also has a partnership in nearby Mill Road and Steinbeck vineyards, which retain 20 percent of the harvest for Eberle wines and sell the remainder to other vintners. Over the decades, Eberle wines have earned more than three hundred gold medals, many of which are on display in the spacious California ranch–style visitor center overlooking one of Paso Robles's oldest and most legendary vineyards.

# HALTER RANCH VINEYARD

Located on a thousand acres just west of Paso Robles, Halter Ranch Vineyard has been part of a working ranch since 1880. With its farmhouse, mature orchards, and vintage outbuildings, it continues to offer a taste of old California. At the end of the driveway, the restored Victorian farmhouse stands among towering oaks, cottage gardens, and sixty-year-old olive trees. The two-story house, with its red roof and period detailing, glows pale yellow in the dappled shade. Nearby, an enlarged carriage house serves as the tasting room. Inside, open beams enhance the impression of an elegant cabin fitted with a cork floor and curved cherrywood tasting bar. Broad windows are set into one side, and clear glass in a gabled end admits extra light. Two sets of french doors open onto a patio beside Las Tablas Creek. Beyond the tasting room, a collection of nineteenth-century barns and grain silos remains as evidence of a long agricultural tradition.

A covered bridge spanning the creek leads to the estate's magnificent 34,000-square-foot winery, completed in 2011. Clad in cedar siding, the winery resembles the old barns on the ranch, but with a chaletlike flavor in keeping with owner Hansjörg Wyss's Swiss roots. Copper gutters flash in the sun, and portions of the exterior walls are faced with Adelaida stone taken from the property and cut on-site. The state-of-the-art facility stands on a hill 1,600 feet in elevation and embraces a number of green features, including a cooling system that automatically draws in chilly night air. It also boasts a gravity flow system that gently transports juice throughout the winery, yielding exceptional wine. Underground, 20,000 square feet of recently constructed caves offer cool, naturally insulated space for aging wine-filled barrels.

Just beyond the winery's landscaped beds of lavender and drought-tolerant grasses grow Cabernet Sauvignon, Grenache, and Syrah, part of the estate's 280 acres of grapes. The vineyards are planted to twenty different varieties, many of which are farmed with no supplemental irrigation. To help control pests, chickens roam the rows by day, returning at dusk to their mobile coop, which is equipped with a solar-powered gate. The vineyards are all Sustainability in Practice (SIP) certified, having met standards set by the Central Coast Vineyard Team in areas such as water conservation, energy efficiency, and labor relations. Primarily Rhône- and Bordeaux-style blends, the wines are 100 percent estate grown and also SIP certified. The Estate Reserve red blend, called Ancestor, is named for a massive, centuries-old live oak growing near the vineyard, a living reminder of the property's long history and a harbinger of its promising future.

**HALTER RANCH VINEYARD**
8910 Adelaida Rd.
Paso Robles, CA 93446
805-226-9455
info@halterranch.com
www.halterranch.com

**OWNER:** Hansjörg Wyss.

**LOCATION:** 9 miles northwest of the intersection of Hwy. 46 West and Vineyard Dr.

**APPELLATION:** Paso Robles.

**HOURS:** 11 A.M.–5 P.M. daily.

**TASTINGS:** $10 for 6 or 7 wines (applicable to purchase).

**TOURS:** By appointment.

**THE WINES:** Cabernet Sauvignon, Grenache Rosé, Sauvignon Blanc, Syrah, Viognier.

**SPECIALTIES:** Ancestor (Bordeaux-style blend), Côtes de Paso (red Rhône-style blend), Côtes de Paso Blanc (white Rhône-style blend).

**WINEMAKER:** Kevin Sass.

**ANNUAL PRODUCTION:** 10,000 cases.

**OF SPECIAL NOTE:** Picnic snacks available on-site. Picnic area located in garden outside tasting room. Winery is pet friendly. Annual summer solstice dinner. Single-variety wines available only in tasting room. A registered champion coast live oak, one of the two largest specimens in the U.S., stands in the middle of one vineyard.

**NEARBY ATTRACTIONS:** Mt. Olive Organic Farm (tours, olive oil tasting, bakery, lunch menu); Pasolivo Olive Oil (olive oil tasting, specialty salts, vinegar, and lotions, picnicking).

# HAMMERSKY VINEYARDS

**HAMMERSKY VINEYARDS**
7725 Vineyard Dr.
Paso Robles, CA 93446
805-239-0930
tastingroom@hammersky.
com
www.hammersky.com

**OWNERS:** Doug and Kim Hauck.

**LOCATION:** 5 miles northwest of the intersection of Hwy. 46 West and Vineyard Dr.

**APPELLATION:** Paso Robles.

**HOURS:** 11 A.M.–5 P.M. Thursday–Sunday.

**TASTINGS:** $10 for 3–5 wines; $15 for 2 reserve wines.

**TOURS:** None.

**THE WINES:** Cabernet Franc, Cabernet Sauvignon, Merlot, Petit Verdot, Zinfandel.

**SPECIALTIES:** Bordeaux-centric blends, Merlot, Zinfandel.

**WINEMAKER:** Doug Hauck.

**ANNUAL PRODUCTION:** 1,800 cases.

**OF SPECIAL NOTE:** Wines are 90 percent estate grown, live music and food on spring and summer weekends. Property includes a 4-bedroom inn open year-around. Red Handed (100 percent Merlot) available in tasting room only.

**NEARBY ATTRACTIONS:** Mt. Olive Organic Farm (tours, olive oil tasting, bakery, lunch menu); Pasolivo Olive Oil (olive oil tasting, specialty salts, vinegar, and lotions, picnicking).

**B**uilt for a Mennonite minister and his family, the gleaming white house at HammerSky Vineyards dates to 1904. When Douglas Hauck and his wife, Kim, bought the fifty-acre property in 2007, they converted the colonial-style gem into a luxurious inn. Despite the home's age, its crisp black shutters, second-floor balcony, and cropped boxwood hedge reveal a contemporary aesthetic. The couple oriented windows to incorporate views of a centuries-old valley oak, affectionately known as Uncle Dan, and erected a post-and-beam Yankee barn behind the house for winery events.

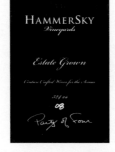

The Haucks farm twenty-five acres of grapes at HammerSky Vineyards, which they named for their two young sons, Hamilton and Skyler. Planted in 1997, the vines grow in soil that compares favorably with that of France's Bordeaux region. A combination of shale, clay loam, and calcareous sandstone, the soil harbors moisture, encouraging the vines to root deeply, and imparts a balanced minerality to the finished wine.

While Kim runs the inn, Doug is involved in all aspects of the wine business, including marketing, vineyard management, and blending stylish wines that he considers couture for the senses. A man of diverse interests, Doug earned a business degree from the University of Southern California, a film degree from the University of California, Los Angeles, and, in 1988, a doctorate of dental surgery from San Francisco's University of the Pacific. He taught dental courses at USC, ran a successful practice in Beverly Hills for two decades, and has enjoyed side careers as a movie producer and Internet entrepreneur. Doug continues to maintain his practice in Orange County, where he counts sports, music, and film celebrities among his clients.

The Haucks' eclectic sense of style is especially evident in the tasting room, which stands at the edge of a parklike lawn dotted with white oaks and picnic tables. The clean lines and smooth, steel-troweled walls of the snow-white structure create a bold impact amid the rural setting. The building, a melding of the refined esthetics of both Doug and Kim Hauck, is just under a thousand square feet and includes an airy space for wine tasting, as well as a barrel room splashed with red and black accents. Tall windows and glass doors admit natural light, while allowing sweeping views of the Merlot vines that border the lawn and café-style seating on the patio. A rough-hewn rectangular table doubles as a tasting bar. To provide at-a-glance information about the wine, Doug created Sensory Integrated Profiling, a visual graph based on the tasting criteria of swirl, sniff, sip, and savor. Individual profiles appear on the back of each bottle, adding a contemporary twist to the old-fashioned pleasures of wine tasting.

# HEARTHSTONE VINEYARD & WINERY

From its hilltop vantage point, Hearthstone Vineyard offers sweeping westward views of neighboring farms and the Santa Lucia Mountains. Mature pines and live oaks shade the wooded site, and a weathered fertilizer wagon in the parking area hints at the region's agrarian history. Opened in 2009, the earth-toned tasting room sports a concrete crush pad and two arched redwood doors that reveal the building's original function as a small private winery. Stones excavated from the property and set into the lower portion of the exterior wall give the structure the look of a mountain house. At  the entry, spiral juniper topiaries flank three glass panels, two of which open into the tasting room. Above the panels, a fan-light bears the winery's sinuous logo, a Gaelic-spirited swirl of smoke rising from an unseen hearth. Inside the square room, gray concrete flooring meets corrugated tin wainscoting that matches the front of the tasting bar. Behind the oak-topped bar, wine bottles and a vineyard scene are mounted on a curved partition of similar corrugated tin.

In fair weather, visitors can sample wine on the patio in front of the tasting room, an ideal spot to enjoy spectacular sunsets. A transparent windbreak shelters the patio from cool ocean air funneled through a series of notches—collectively known as the Templeton Gap—in the Santa Lucia Mountains. The breezes moderate temperatures on the hill and in the vineyard, located eight miles northeast. The forty-acre vineyard grows at 1,400 feet elevation and in shallow calcareous soil, conditions that limit vine production to light crops of small grapes with highly concentrated flavors.

Owner Hoy Buell, a horticulturist and graduate of Cal Poly San Luis Obispo, is a cofounder of Greenheart Farms, one of the nation's largest wholesale nurseries. He had been propagating vines for other growers when, in 1999, he heeded the siren call to plant his own vineyard. Buell sustainably farms twenty different grape varieties, selects about half of the crop for his estate wines, and sells the rest to local winemakers. Given the wide variety of grapes and their limited yields, winemaker Paul Ayers makes small lots of unique blends. Harvest is done clone by clone, and each two-ton batch of fruit is fermented separately. A twenty-eight-year veteran, Ayers honed his craft at a number of the region's pioneer wineries, including Estrella River Winery and Castoro Cellars. When not tending the wines, which are made at a neighboring facility, he often can be found helping out in the tasting room or chatting with visitors over a glass of one of his blends.

**HEARTHSTONE VINEYARD & WINERY**
5070 Vineyard Dr.
Paso Robles, CA 93446
805-238-2544
info@hearthstonevineyard.com
www.hearthstonevineyard.com

**OWNER:** Hoy Buell.

**LOCATION:** 2 miles northwest of the intersection of Hwy. 46 West and Vineyard Dr.

**APPELLATION:** Paso Robles.

**HOURS:** 11 A.M.–5 P.M. Thursday–Monday.

**TASTINGS:** $10 for 7 wines (applicable to purchase).

**TOURS:** None.

**THE WINES:** Cabernet Franc, Cabernet Sauvignon, Grenache, Mourvèdre, Petite Sirah, Pinot Noir, Roussanne, Sangiovese, Syrah, Tempranillo, Viognier, Zinfandel.

**SPECIALTIES:** Rhône- and Bordeaux-style blends, small-lot proprietary blends.

**WINEMAKER:** Paul Ayers.

**ANNUAL PRODUCTION:** 1,500 cases.

**OF SPECIAL NOTE:** All wines are estate grown and sold primarily out of the tasting room. Live music and food pairings monthly. Educational seminars quarterly.

**NEARBY ATTRACTIONS:** Mt. Olive Organic Farm (tours, olive and olive oil tasting, bakery, lunch menu); Pasolivo Olive Oil (olive oil tasting, specialty vinegars, salts, and lotions, picnicking).

# J. LOHR VINEYARDS & WINES

**J. LOHR VINEYARDS & WINES**
6169 Airport Rd.
Paso Robles, CA 93446
805-239-8900
prwinecenter@jlohr.com
www.jlohr.com

**OWNER:** Jerry Lohr.

**LOCATION:** 6 miles east of downtown Paso Robles.

**APPELLATION:** Paso Robles.

**HOURS:** 10 A.M.–5 P.M. daily.

**TASTINGS:** No fee, except for the Cuvée Series trio of wines and the limited-production wines ($5), available Friday, Saturday, and Sunday only.

**TOURS:** None.

**THE WINES:** Cabernet Sauvignon, Chardonnay, Grenache, Merlot, Mourvèdre, Petite Sirah, Pinot Noir, Riesling, Sauvignon Blanc, Syrah, Valdiguié, Viognier, Zinfandel.

**SPECIALTIES:** Cuvée Series (Bordeaux-style blends), Gesture series (Rhône-inspired blends and varieties).

**WINEMAKERS:** Jeff Meier, director of winemaking; Steve Peck, red winemaker.

**ANNUAL PRODUCTION:** 1.25 million cases.

**OF SPECIAL NOTE:** Cookbooks, culinary and wine accessories, and items crafted by local artisans sold in tasting room. Rhône-inspired Gesture series available in tasting room only. The original J. Lohr San Jose Wine Center is open daily, 10 A.M.–5 P.M.

**NEARBY ATTRACTIONS:** Estrella Warbird Museum (restored military aircraft); Centennial Park (playground, picnic area, walking paths).

Raised on a South Dakota farm, Jerry Lohr enjoyed successful careers as a civil engineer and custom home builder. A passion for wine, however, drove him back to his agricultural roots. In the late 1960s, Lohr began scouting California's Central Coast for vineyard sites. He took viticulture and enology classes at U.C. Davis and in 1973 planted a 280-acre vineyard in Monterey County. A year later he opened a winery in San Jose that produced popular wines at affordable prices. Stimulated by the challenges of the wine industry, Lohr planted a vineyard near Sacramento and purchased a thirty-five-acre vineyard in Napa Valley. Determining that Paso Robles would be ideal for growing red grapes, he planted Cabernet Sauvignon vines about six miles north of the city in 1986 and became one of Paso  Robles' viticultural pioneers. Two years later, Lohr built a winery and barrel room near his vineyard.

Confident in the region's potential for producing superior fruit, Lohr eventually planted more than 3,000 acres of vines in the Paso Robles appellation. It was a heavy commitment, but with the 1989 launch of his J. Lohr Estates wines featuring all-estate fruit, Lohr elevated his label to a new level of quality. In 2002 he launched the heralded J. Lohr Cuvée Series, a trio of blended red wines made in the styles of the Bordeaux regions of Pauillac, St. Emilion, and Pomerol. Debuting in 2009, the Gesture series of Rhône-inspired wines reflects the distinctive microclimates of western Paso Robles. Both series are produced in limited quantities.

Jerry Lohr has long been active in the wine industry. He has been recognized for his many contributions, most recently in 2011, when he received the prestigious Lifetime Achievement Award from the California Association of Winegrape Growers. Lohr, with his winegrowing and farming expertise, and his experienced winemaking team—Jeff Meier, director of winemaking, who has been with the winery for thirty years, and red winemaker Steve Peck—enjoy a productive partnership whose consistency and attention to detail have brought acclaim to the J. Lohr portfolio of wines.

Lohr's three grown children, Steve, Cynthia, and Lawrence, hold executive positions in the family business. In 2009 the Lohrs unveiled a three-acre solar tracking array located behind the Paso Robles winery, the largest winery-based solar array of its kind in North America. Visitors to the J. Lohr Paso Robles Wine Center are greeted by a boulder of local limestone chiseled with the winery's name. A wraparound veranda set with teak tables and chairs offers views of the Cabernet Sauvignon vines that Lohr planted a quarter of a century ago.

# JUSTIN VINEYARDS & WINERY

Cattle dominated the rangeland in 1981 when Justin Baldwin purchased 160 acres west of Paso Robles. With funds for a modest venture, he planted 72 acres of Bordeaux-type vines. At the time, his was the westernmost vineyard in a region with only nine wineries. Baldwin, a well-traveled investment banker, had enjoyed many fine vintages with clients and boldly resolved to make wines comparable to the first growths of Bordeaux. In 1987, four years after he helped establish the Paso Robles appellation, Baldwin debuted his flagship wine. A Bordeaux-style blend, it was called Isosceles, in reference to its three constituents of Cabernet Sauvignon, Cabernet Franc, and Merlot.

By 1996, Baldwin had built a state-of-the-art winery complex on the property. A year later, at the London International Wine and Spirits Competition, the 1994 Isosceles was named the world's best blended red Bordeaux-style wine, a coup that put Justin Vineyards—and Paso Robles—on the international wine map. In 2003 the winery completed 18,000 square feet of caves for storing 5,000 barrels. At the deepest part of the caves, 120 feet below ground, lies the Isosceles Library, which is featured on winery tours. Niches in the gunite walls hold past vintages, liquid histories that track the progress of Baldwin's maturing estate vineyard. All tours include a visit to the caves.

Lying thirteen miles from the Pacific Ocean, the vineyard grows at elevations ranging between 1,200 and 1,800 feet. Farming practices include the use of nitrogen-fixing cover crops between rows and biodynamic preparations for healthy soil. In 2012, shortly after Stewart and Lynda Resnick purchased the winery, new Cabernet Sauvignon vines were planted around the tasting room. In front of the tasting room, black walnut trees shade a pet-friendly picnic area complete with redwood tables, leash tethers, and water bowls. Low walls of local stone define a small demonstration vineyard, and a shaded portico encircles an English garden maze boasting a fountain, roses, and manicured boxwood hedges.

On a sheltered patio, visitors can order lunch on Saturdays from the winery's restaurant. Gourmet dinners are served in an intimate dining area off the tasting room lobby, where staff members welcome guests wishing to dine or taste wine. Lining the wide hall to the tasting room, diamond-shaped shelves of cherry-stained pine hold hundreds of bottles of wine. Painted in warm tones of saffron and terra-cotta, the tasting room has two tasting bars fashioned from cherry-hued wood and topped with copper. Hanging behind one bar, a tapestry with a wine scene lends rich texture to a modest space that originally served as the winery's barrel room.

**JUSTIN VINEYARDS & WINERY**
11680 Chimney Rock Rd.
Paso Robles, CA 93446
805-238-6932
info@justinwine.com
www.justinwine.com

**OWNER:** Fiji Water.

**LOCATION:** 13 miles northwest of the intersection of Hwy. 46 West and Vineyard Dr.

**APPELLATION:** Paso Robles.

**HOURS:** 10 A.M. – 5 P.M. daily.

**TASTINGS:** $10 for 5–7 wines; barrel tasting, $30, 3:30 P.M. daily, with reservation 24 hours in advance.

**TOURS:** Winery and cave tours ($15), 10:30 A.M., 2:30 P.M., and 3:30 P.M. daily, include tasting in caves.

**THE WINES:** Cabernet Sauvignon, Chardonnay, Sauvignon Blanc, Syrah, Tempranillo, Viognier.

**SPECIALTIES:** Isosceles (Cabernet Sauvignon, Cabernet Franc, Merlot), Savant (Syrah, Cabernet Sauvignon), Justification (Cabernet Franc, Merlot), Focus (Syrah, Grenache).

**WINEMAKER:** Scott Shirley.

**ANNUAL PRODUCTION:** 85,000 cases.

**OF SPECIAL NOTE:** Educational wine seminars in summer. Tasting room stocks light snacks, books, and wine accessories. Restaurant serves dinner Tuesday – Sunday, lunch on Saturdays. A bed-and-breakfast inn is on-site. Reserve Cabernet Sauvignon, Reserve Tempranillo, Petit Verdot, Malbec, and Zinfandel available only in tasting room.

**NEARBY ATTRACTION:** Pismo State Beach (swimming, hiking, camping).

# LAETITIA VINEYARD & WINERY

**LAETITIA VINEYARD & WINERY**
453 Laetitia Vineyard Dr.
Arroyo Grande, CA 93420
805-474-7651
888-809-VINE
www.laetitiawine.com

**OWNER:** Selim Zilkha.

**LOCATION:** Directly off U.S.
101, between the towns of
Nipomo and Pismo Beach.

**APPELLATION:** Arroyo
Grande Valley.

**HOURS:** 11 A.M.–5 P.M. daily.

**TASTINGS:** $10 for 5 wines;
$10 for 5 reserve wines.

**TOURS:** None.

**THE WINES:** Brut Cuvée and
Brut Rosé sparkling wines,
Cabernet, Chardonnay,
Pinot Noir, Syrah.

**SPECIALTIES:** Estate Pinot
Noir, *méthode champenoise*
sparkling wines.

**WINEMAKERS:** Eric Hickey
(still wines); Dave Hickey
(sparkling wines).

**ANNUAL PRODUCTION:**
60,000 cases.

**OF SPECIAL NOTE:** Visitors
can see fully operational
press room. Five picnic
areas with umbrellas;
bocce ball court on-site.
Gift shop offering clothing,
stemware, and books.
Select Pinot Noirs and
Barnwood wines from
Santa Barbara Highlands
vineyard available only in
tasting room.

**NEARBY ATTRACTIONS:**
Arroyo Grande Village
(Old West downtown with
historic walking tour);
Pismo State Beach (swim-
ming, hiking, camping).

The stunning views from the hilltop decks at Laetitia Vineyard & Winery rival the best on the Central Coast: a panorama of vineyards, the pastoral Arroyo Grande Valley, and the Pacific Ocean, just three miles to the west. In 1982 this gorgeous site captivated French viticulturists from Champagne Deutz, the esteemed Champagne house, who were searching for a suitable location to grow grapes and produce *méthode champenoise* sparkling wines in the United States. The viticulturalists were also impressed with the property's volcanic soils and climates, which resembled those in their native Epernay, France, and would promote high acid and minerality. They planted 185 acres to Pinot Noir, Chardonnay, and Pinot Blanc in specific sites chosen for their soil profile, exposure, and microclimate, and established Maison Deutz, a winery that quickly earned a reputation for outstanding sparkling wines.

In 1997 vineyard owner chased Maison Deutz and after his daughter. The win-sparkling wine to still wine style varieties, and experimen-potential as a premier site for Jean-Claude Tardivat pur-renamed the winery Laetitia ery's focus began to shift from production of Burgundian-tation revealed the vineyards' growing Pinot Noir. A year later, the winery was acquired by a partnership that included Selim Zilkha. In 2001 Zilkha obtained sole proprietorship of Laetitia.

Today the 1,800-acre Laetitia ranch includes 620 acres of vineyard blocks, with 430 acres devoted to Pinot Noir. Laetitia also owns a second vineyard, Santa Barbara Highlands, at a 3,200-foot elevation, sixty miles inland in the Cuyama Valley. This vineyard grows mostly Bordeaux varieties for Laetitia's Barnwood and NADIA portfolio of wines. The Hickey family manages nearly all day-to-day winery business. Winemaker Eric Hickey, who has worked at the winery since 1990, directs the still wine production and vineyard operations. Eric's father, Dave Hickey, began his career at Maison Deutz in 1985. He continues the winery's French tradition by making sparkling wines in the *champenoise* method, producing bubbles during a secondary fermentation in the bottle rather than in barrels. Eric's mother, Carmen, manages the tasting room, and his brother, Dustin, helps out in the cellar.

Visitors to the casual, country-style tasting room can view the adjacent press room, which houses two rare Coquard wooden basket presses, made in France, that Dave Hickey uses to press estate-grown Pinot Noir, Chardonnay, and Pinot Blanc grapes. These are the only such presses operated in the United States. Outdoors, visitors can relax in Adirondack chairs under yellow and white umbrellas on a lawn, above the gravity-flow winery and sweeping scenes of the ocean beyond.

# MONDO CELLARS

Located atop a chaparral-covered hill, the Mondo Cellars tasting room offers a bird's-eye view of the farmland just west of Paso Robles. Painted a soft adobe pink, it bears design elements inspired by the architecture of Tuscany. Double entry doors are made of knotty alder and framed with gray Verona Hillstone applied to the exterior wall. Pillars faced with similar stone support a roof that partially covers the patio, which is set with cast aluminum tables and chairs that can accommodate more than a hundred people. For all-weather comfort, there are festive brick red canvas umbrellas, outdoor heaters, and a gas-fueled fire pit. Visitors can relax on the patio and drink in the spectacular view, while enjoying seated tastings served by staff members.

Winery owners Mitch and Doug Mondo offer seated tastings as a gesture of hospitality. Half Italian and half Scottish, the brothers honor their father's Sicilian heritage by providing a welcoming environment where visitors can relish both the wines and the scenery. Originally from Southern California, they have run their own companies since they were in their early twenties. The pair first partnered in the early 1980s in a production company that videotaped depositions and legal proceedings, and later founded several other enterprises. For fun, the brothers often visited San Luis Obispo County to explore wine country. In 1991 they bought land west of Paso Robles as a vacation getaway. Longtime wine collectors, the pair eventually sold their companies to finance their own winery.

In 2004 they moved permanently to Paso Robles and four years later began converting a pair of buildings on their eighty-two-acre property into a winery and tasting room. Wanting to specialize in Rhone- and Bordeaux-style blends, the brothers purchased fruit from vineyards in Santa Barbara, San Luis Obispo, and Monterey counties. They released their first wine in 2009. That same year, they opened the 1,142-square-foot tasting room, where the interior peach-colored walls cast soft light over a rustic floor made of oil-rubbed oak. The bar, a reclaimed four-inch-thick slab of Douglas fir, rests atop retired wine barrels. Wrought iron shirt racks and room dividers lend an old-world touch to the intimate space. For sale in shades of tan, gray, and black, fedoras festoon the walls, lighthearted reminders of the Mondos' Sicilian heritage and their playful regard of visitors as family members.

**MONDO CELLARS**
3260 Lake Nacimiento Dr.
Paso Robles, CA 93446
805-226-2925
jmmondo@mondocellars.com
www.mondocellars.com

**OWNERS:** Doug and Mitch Mondo.

**LOCATION:** 5 miles west of the intersection of U.S. 101 and 24th St.

**APPELLATION:** Paso Robles.

**HOURS:** 11 A.M.–5 P.M. daily in winter; 11 A.M.–6 P.M. daily in summer.

**TASTINGS:** $5 for 5–7 wines (applicable to purchase).

**TOURS:** Self-guided.

**THE WINES:** Cabernet Franc, Cabernet Sauvignon, Grenache, Grenache Blanc, Marsanne, Merlot, Mourvèdre, Petite Sirah, Roussanne, Syrah, Zinfandel.

**SPECIALTIES:** Red Bordeaux- and Rhône-style blends.

**WINEMAKER:** Kevin Riley.

**ANNUAL PRODUCTION:** 2,000 cases.

**OF SPECIAL NOTE:** Tasting room is pet friendly. Friday night Sunset Happy Hour, 5–9 P.M., March through October. Three-suite bed-and-breakfast inn on-site. All wines available in tasting room only.

**NEARBY ATTRACTIONS:** Mt. Olive Organic Farm (tours, olive oil tasting, bakery, lunch menu); Pasolivo Olive Oil (olive oil tasting, specialty salts, vinegar, and lotions, picnicking).

# NINER WINE ESTATES

**NINER WINE ESTATES**
2400 Highway 46 West
Paso Robles, CA 93446
805-239-2233
info@ninerwine.com
www.ninerwine.com

**OWNERS:** Pam and Dick Niner.

**LOCATION:** 2.5 miles from downtown Paso Robles.

**APPELLATION:** Paso Robles.

**HOURS:** 10 A.M.–5 P.M. daily.

**TASTINGS:** $10 for 5 or 6 wines.

**TOURS:** None.

**THE WINES:** Cabernet Franc, Cabernet Sauvignon, Grenache Blanc, Malbec, Merlot, Petite Sirah, Sangiovese, Sauvignon Blanc, Syrah.

**SPECIALTIES:** Cabernet Sauvignon, Fog Catcher (proprietary red Bordeaux-style blend).

**WINEMAKER:** Amanda Cramer.

**ANNUAL PRODUCTION:** 14,000 cases.

**OF SPECIAL NOTE:** All wines are estate grown. Picnic tables on view terrace. Cooking classes held in a commercial-grade kitchen, farmers' market forays, educational seminars, and wine-and-cheese pairings scheduled throughout the year. Cheese, crackers, and the winery's own olive oil, as well as wine accessories, sold in the hospitality center.

**NEARBY ATTRACTIONS:** Templeton Park (events including weekly summer concerts and farmers' market); Jack Creek Farms (demonstration gardens, pick-your-own-produce, May–November).

Vineyards and barley fields grace the fringes of Niner Wine Estates, located on Heart Hill, named for a naturally shaped grove of oak trees. Set amid beds of white Meidiland roses and French lavender, the hospitality center and boutique winery suggest an elegant, old-world farmstead. Built in 2010, the barnlike structures sport steeply pitched roofs and cut-stone walls. Despite the traditional appearance, they represent the latest in green building practices, including the use of rainfall catchment systems and recycled materials. Inside the hospitality center is an octagonal tasting bar with a gleaming copper top. Pendant lights illuminate the bar and a casual seating area.

Proprietors Pam and Dick Niner founded the winery in 2001, after purchasing Bootjack Ranch, 150 acres of primarily Rhône- and Bordeaux-type grapes located nine miles east of Paso Robles. In 2003 the couple acquired Heart Hill, west of U.S. 101, where they planted nine varieties on 46 acres. Eight years later, they bought a 112-acre ranch in Edna Valley, complete with 39 acres of wine grapes, south of San Luis Obispo.

Pam hails from New York City, and Dick, a graduate of Harvard Business School, grew up in rural West Virginia. When the business of turning around small companies brought the pair to San Luis Obispo County in 1996, Dick felt at home among the vineyards and cattle ranches. The couple decided to put down roots and promptly established a winery that soon became noted for culinary and wine appreciation programs, as well as quality wines.

Winemaker Amanda Cramer, who advised the Niners on which grape varieties to plant, attended U.C. Davis, then worked at several celebrated Northern California wineries, including Far Niente and Paradigm Winery. Hired at Niner in 2004 and charged with helping to design the production facility, Cramer canvassed colleagues in Napa Valley to configure the perfect winery. The resulting 60,000-square-foot state-of-the art facility includes a gravity-fed system that gently moves fruit and juice, yielding superior wine; circular arrays of fermentation tanks for seamless transport of must; and catwalks for easy access to tank tops. In the 2010 San Francisco International Wine Competition, Cramer received the coveted André Tchelistcheff Winemaker of the Year award.

In 2011 Niner Wine Estates became the first Central Coast winery to earn LEED certification from the U.S. Green Building Council. An acronym for Leadership in Energy and Environmental Design, LEED promotes sustainable building and recognizes excellence in green construction practices. Based upon superior performance in areas of energy efficiency, sustainable site development, and indoor environmental quality, Niner Wine Estates received the prestigious LEED Silver rating.

# Opolo Vineyards

Heading through the gate at Opolo Vineyards, visitors enter a viticultural wonderland anchored by an unassuming tasting room: a converted tractor barn decorated to inspire guests to relax and have fun. Famed for its loyal fans and weekend festivities, often featuring grilled delicacies—from sausage and lamb to Cevapcici, a Serbian-style roll of minced beef—this event-driven destination serves up a lively mix of food, wine, and convivial pleasure. Guests can sip wine on the covered deck while taking in the vineyard views, or they can step inside, where giant posters brighten the walls and stacked barrels share space with cases of wine. At wooden planks laid atop oak barrels, friendly staffers pour the listed wines, and then, based on each taster's preferences, suggest others from the winery's thirty-some offerings.

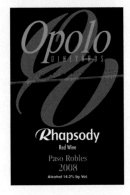

Opolo Vineyards owners, Rick Quinn and David Nichols, share the winemaking duties and welcome feedback from the staff, information that they feel helps them produce wines with the widest customer appeal. When evaluating potential blends, they sometimes even ask tasting room visitors to weigh in on the decision.

A software developer and owner of a real estate brokerage, Quinn first made wine with his family in Minnesota. He revived the tradition when he moved to Southern California, where his successes inspired Nichols, his neighbor and the proprietor of a wireless electronics firm, to take up the hobby. In 1995, when Quinn's Merlot source dried up, the dynamic businessman planted his own vineyard on the west side of Paso Robles with an eye toward supplying his home winemaking needs and selling the rest of the crop to commercial producers. Two years later, Nichols bought the vineyard next to Quinn's and the two plunged into the grape-growing business, selling their fruit to such respected Napa Valley cellars as Niebaum-Coppola, St. Supéry, Fetzer, and Hess Collection. Today they farm three hundred acres of vineyards on the west and east side and continue to sell fruit to some of the finest wineries in the state.

In 1998 the partners noted an industry-wide surplus of grapes and began making wine under their own label in a bid to showcase their vineyards' quality and enhance grape sales. The partners bottled some Merlot, labeling half "Merlot" and the other half "Opolo," the name of a Dalmatian Coast wine selected to honor Quinn's heritage. Believing the wines to be different, friends overwhelmingly preferred the latter, making Opolo, in Nichols's words, the "slam dunk" choice for the name of their new enterprise. Ten years and thousands of cases later, the partners have created a viticultural destination with a well-earned reputation for treating visitors to a good time.

**Opolo Vineyards**
7110 Vineyard Dr.
Paso Robles, CA 93446
805-238-9593
sales@opolo.com
www.opolo.com

**Owners:** Rick Quinn, David Nichols.

**Location:** 8 miles west of U.S. 101.

**Appellation:** Paso Robles.

**Hours:** 10 a.m.–5 p.m. daily.

**Tastings:** $5.

**Tours:** By appointment.

**The Wines:** Cabernet Sauvignon, Chardonnay, Grenache, Malbec, Merlot, Mourvèdre, Muscat Canelli, Petit Verdot, Petite Sirah, Pinot Grigio, Pinot Noir, Roussanne, Sangiovese, Syrah, Tempranillo, Viognier, Zinfandel.

**Specialties:** Montagna-Mare (Barbera, Sangiovese blend), Mountain Zinfandel, Rhapsody (Merlot, Cabernet Sauvignon, Petit Verdot blend).

**Winemakers:** Rick Quinn, David Nichols.

**Annual Production:** 40,000 cases.

**Of Special Note:** On-site bed-and-breakfast, The Inn at Opolo. Harvest grape stomp and various weekend events.

**Nearby Attraction:** Mt. Olive Organic Farm (tours, olive and olive oil tasting, bakery, lunch menu).

# PEACHY CANYON WINERY

**PEACHY CANYON WINERY**
1480 N. Bethel Rd.
Templeton, CA 93465
805-239-1918
866-335-1918
tastingroom@
peachycanyon.com
www.peachycanyon.com

**OWNERS:** Doug and
Nancy Beckett, Josh
and Jake Beckett.

**LOCATION:** Just off Hwy.
46 West, 1.5 miles west of
U.S. 101.

**APPELLATION:** Paso Robles.

**HOURS:** 11 A.M.–5 P.M. daily.
Extended hours in summer.

**TASTINGS:** $5 for 6 wines
(applicable to purchase).

**TOURS:** By appointment.

**THE WINES:** Cabernet
Franc, Cabernet Sauvi-
gnon, Merlot, Petite Sirah,
Viognier, Zinfandel.

**SPECIALTY:** Zinfandel.

**WINEMAKER:** Josh Beckett.

**ANNUAL PRODUCTION:**
75,000 cases.

**OF SPECIAL NOTE:**
Locally made condiments,
home accessories, and gift
items sold in tasting room.
Picnic area overlooking
vineyard. A rental guest
cottage nearby is available
for wine country stays.
Zinfandel Port-style wine
and limited production
wines available only in
tasting room.

**NEARBY ATTRACTIONS:**
Templeton Park (events
including weekly summer
concerts); Jack Creek
Farms (demonstration
gardens, pick-your-own
produce, May–November).

A fine example of old Paso Robles architecture, the Peachy Canyon Winery tasting room was built in 1886 as a country schoolhouse. The white clapboard building features a red brick chimney and lattice-covered deck. It stands amid a lush lawn with valley oaks and an old-fashioned gazebo. Colorful canvas umbrellas shade white picnic tables, and table grape vines border the walkway to the tasting room. Near the front door, the basket press used in 1988 to make Peachy Canyon's first wine serves as a reminder of humble beginnings.

In 1982 Doug and Nancy Beckett left teaching careers in Southern California and moved to Paso Robles to raise their children in a more rural environment. A short time later, Doug joined the ranks of home winemakers, crafting Zinfandel by night in five-gallon water bottles. He used a pitchfork to scoop grapes into a portable crusher and borrowed barrels from a friend. When the harvest ended, Doug was certain that winemaking was his calling.

The Becketts purchased their first Zinfandel grapes from the locally renowned Dusi Vineyard. Since then, the family has established four estate vineyards totaling a hundred acres: the Snow, Mustang Springs, Old School House, and Mustard Creek vineyards. All have earned Sustainability in Practice certification, which requires growers to meet rigorous standards in such areas as habitat conservation, energy efficiency, and labor relations. Each vineyard includes a block or more of Zinfandel, the winery's signature variety. Active members of the national Zinfandel Advocates and Producers, the Becketts maintain an experimental planting of Zinfandel at their Mustang Springs Vineyard, nine miles north of the tasting room. This planting is part of the U.C. Davis Heritage Project, which supports Zinfandel research and preservation of the special qualities of the increasingly rare old vines.

The winery is a family affair involving both of the Becketts' sons. Josh, who has worked at the winery since 1998, became the winemaker in 2003. His younger brother, Jake, apprenticed as vineyard manager before becoming general sales manager in 2005. Gracing many of the wine labels is an image of the distinctive two-story house on Peachy Canyon Road that the Becketts once called home. They chose the image as a familiar reference point that would reinforce the label's regional identity, but the story of the winery's name goes a little deeper into local color. According to reliable lore, an old horse thief whose surname was Peachy used to hide out with his four-legged booty in bat caves concealed amid the rugged outcroppings of Paso Robles' west side. The last member of the Peachy family, a dentist, left the area years ago, but the legend and the singular name live on.

# PENMAN SPRINGS VINEYARD

Penman Springs Vineyard stands on a broad rise overlooking vineyards, oak savannas, and sculpted hills. Although the rural scenery and country solitude suggest a more remote spot, the winery is located just three miles east of downtown Paso Robles. A short driveway curves past the winery's vineyard and ends at the tasting room, which faces blocks of Petite Sirah and gnarled Cabernet Sauvignon vines.

To encourage visitors to take in the spectacular view while enjoying a picnic lunch, owners Beth and Carl McCasland have placed concrete tables and benches beside the tasting room. Entering the white board-and-batten building, visitors find a homey space, complete with an upright piano, a pellet-burning stove, and a table spread with a jigsaw puzzle in progress. As in the early days when Paso Robles tasting rooms were usually staffed by their owners, Beth is often behind the bar. She believes in treating tasters as if they were guests in her home and occasionally pairs Penman Springs wines with artisan breads, meats, and cheeses. After calling out a cheerful greeting, she ensures that tastings are relaxed, educational, and fun. Opened in 2000, the simple tasting room features a cathedral ceiling that lends elegance to the welcoming space. Wine competition ribbons line the walls, and the well-stocked Penman Pantry holds crackers, grape seed and olive oils, vinegars, and chocolate sauces, as well as locally made goat milk soap.

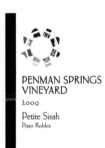

The McCaslands purchased what Carl calls their "garden" in 1996, after selling Sun King Container, a plant they owned in Texas. The forty-acre property included sixteen acres of established grapevines. Doing much of the work himself, Carl replanted more than half of the original vines and expanded the vineyard to thirty-one acres, following sustainable agricultural principles. He installed a variety of trellis systems and continues to manage the grapevine canopies to allow sunshine and warm air to ripen the grapes. Inspiration for this approach came from Dr. Richard Smart's seminal book *Sunlight Into Wine*.

In 1998 the McCaslands hired Larry Roberts as their winemaker and launched the Penman Springs Vineyard brand. Roberts designed the label bearing the image of a distinctive color wheel created from shards of glass by Beth's architect brother. The McCaslands' first crush consisted of Merlot, Cabernet Sauvignon, Muscat Blanc, and purchased Chardonnay. With the production from new vines, they have expanded the line to include Syrah, Petite Sirah, Meritage, occasional Petit Verdot, and fortified dessert wines. The couple continues to work closely with Roberts to craft the wines, which are 100 percent estate grown.

**PENMAN SPRINGS VINEYARD**
1985 Penman Springs Rd.
Paso Robles, CA 93446
805-237-7959
penmansprings@gmail.com
www.penmansprings.com

**OWNERS:** Carl and Beth McCasland.

**LOCATION:** 2.5 miles east of Hwy. 46 East.

**APPELLATION:** Paso Robles.

**HOURS:** 11 A.M.–5 P.M. Thursday–Sunday.

**TASTINGS:** $5 (applicable to purchase).

**TOURS:** None.

**THE WINES:** Cabernet Sauvignon, Meritage, Merlot, Muscat Blanc, Petit Verdot, Petite Sirah, Syrah, fortified wine.

**SPECIALTIES:** Cabernet Sauvignon "Old Block," Meritage "Artisan Cuvée," Penman Reserve, Petite Sirah.

**WINEMAKER:** Larry Roberts.

**ANNUAL PRODUCTION:** 2,400 cases.

**OF SPECIAL NOTE:** Picnic area. Penman Pantry stocks books, local condiments, one-of-a-kind jewelry, and handmade goat milk soap. Late-harvest and fortified wines available only at tasting room.

**NEARBY ATTRACTIONS:** Barney Schwartz Park (lake, picnic areas); Estrella Warbird Museum (restored military aircraft, memorabilia).

# POMAR JUNCTION VINEYARD & WINERY

**POMAR JUNCTION VINEYARD & WINERY**
5036 S. El Pomar Rd.
Templeton, CA 93465
805-238-9940
info@pomarjunction.com
www.pomarjunction.com

**OWNERS:** Dana and Marsha Merrill, Matt and Nicole Merrill.

**LOCATION:** 6 miles east of the intersection of U.S. 101 and Vineyard Dr.

**APPELLATION:** Paso Robles.

**HOURS:** 11 A.M.–5 P.M. daily.

**TASTINGS:** $5 for 5 wines.

**TOURS:** Winery tours on request.

**THE WINES:** Cabernet Sauvignon, Chardonnay, Merlot, Pinot Noir, Syrah, Viognier, Zinfandel.

**SPECIALTIES:** Reserve Cabernet Sauvignon, Train Wreck (red blend of Cabernet Sauvignon, Petite Sirah, Syrah, and Zinfandel).

**WINEMAKER:** Jim Shumate.

**ANNUAL PRODUCTION:** 6,000 cases.

**OF SPECIAL NOTE:** Winery offers horse-drawn carriage tours of the vineyard. Once a month, April through October, Train Wreck Friday ($10, 5:30–8:30 P.M.) features live music. Wine accessories and gift items sold in tasting room.

**NEARBY ATTRACTIONS:** Templeton Park (events including weekly summer concerts, Saturday farmers' market); Jack Creek Farms (demonstration gardens, pick-your-own produce, May–November).

In the late 1880s, the Templeton area was called *el pomar*, Spanish for "the orchard." By 1925, its rolling hills blossomed with some of the largest almond plantings in the world. Today, as vineyards replace the orchards, the area remains quiet, rural, and seemingly remote. A weathered red water tank stands near the intersection of El Pomar Drive and South El Pomar Road, the crossroads that inspired the Merrill family to name their winery Pomar Junction. At the winery's entrance, a wooden water tank and a green, nineteenth-century grain wagon mark the long driveway, which is lined with eighty-year-old almond trees. Resting in their shade are antique agricultural essentials, including a wooden almond hauler.

Dana and Marsha Merrill, and their son, Matthew, represent eight generations of farming on the Central Coast. For thirty years, the family has grown wine grapes and managed vineyards for wineries such as Robert Mondavi. As a charter member of the Central Coast Vineyard Team in the 1990s, Dana helped develop the Sustainability in Practice (SIP) certification program, which fosters sustainable agricultural and business practices by evaluating such elements as water and energy conservation, and labor relations.

In 2002 the Merrills bought the 130-acre Pomar Junction property and planted 91 acres to nearly a dozen different grape varieties. In 2008 the vineyard received SIP certification. The wines, also SIP certified, are made in a warehouse-style winery, built near the vineyard in 2011. Eager to showcase the region's warm hospitality, the Merrills converted a 1920s-era farmhouse on the property into a tasting room. The cottage features redwood arbors and a back deck, as well as a patio with garden beds and a trickling fountain. Inside, a welcoming hodgepodge of rooms has been added on over the years. A well-used brick fireplace graces what was once the living room, where amiable staffers pour wine at a copper-topped bar rescued from an 1880s-vintage Paso Robles saloon. Red oak floors and knotty pine cabinets in the kitchen are original to the house.

Out front, a mature elm tree towers over a lawn dotted with redwood picnic tables, and the driveway ends at a white clapboard shed built in the early 1920s for hulling almonds. Beyond the shed, a retired red boxcar and cupola caboose rest on a length of rail. The abbreviated train honors the Southern Pacific Railroad, which reached Templeton in 1887, as well as Marsha's grandfather, who was an engineer with the line. Picnic tables nearby afford sweeping vineyard views and a comfortable spot for enjoying the historic farmstead, a reminder of bygone days that live on at this inviting family winery.

# Robert Hall Winery

While touring France in the late 1970s, businessman and entrepreneur Robert Hall discovered an appreciation for the wine and lifestyle of the Rhône region. A native Minnesotan, he was drawn to the farming aspects of winemaking, and to the pleasures of wine-and-food pairing. His career had involved successful ventures ranging from commercial construction to the breeding of champion Arabian horses. With this newfound passion for wine, he decided that his next pursuit would be to make food-friendly wines that would enhance any dining table.

In 1995 Hall purchased 160 acres of former barley fields located just east of Paso Robles. He planted the 140-acre Home 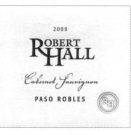 Ranch Vineyard to vines known to suit the *terroir*, including several Bordeaux and a dozen Rhône varieties. Over the years, Hall acquired additional land and extended his planting to include five Portuguese varieties that are used to create a tradi- tional vintage port each year. Given his love of the land and environment, in 2008 all three vineyards earned SIP (Sustain- ability in Practice) certification, which verifies the use of farming practices including pest management and water conservation.

In 1999 Hall built his state-of-the art winery, which includes one of the Central Coast's first underground wine caverns. Natural insulation keeps interior temperatures around sixty degrees Fahrenheit, which is ideal for the 4,000 oak barrels and five 2,000-gallon upright wood tanks filled with wine. Decorative light fixtures—crafted by local students after Hall bought welding equipment for their high school—lend an elegant touch. After completing the caverns and 21,000-square-foot winery, Hall built a stunning hospitality center, which opened in 2005. In front of the center, a foun- tain rises from a brick-walled pool. Water tumbles over the fountain, runs into two reflecting pools, and then cascades over a four-tiered course set amid brick terraces in the open-air amphitheater behind the center.

Framed by a red brick colonnade reminiscent of early Paso Robles architecture, the center has two wings linked by a shaded courtyard. One wing houses the magnificent tasting room, with its forty-foot-high ceiling and massive mahogany and cherrywood tasting bar. In a corner of the room, the gold-painted likeness of a brown bear commemorates the winery's 2010 win of the Golden Winery award at the California State Fair Commercial Wine Competition, the oldest judged wine tasting in North America. The winery was the first Central Coast producer to receive the prestigious award.

**Robert Hall Winery**
3443 Mill Rd.
Paso Robles, CA 93446
805-239-1616
info@roberthallwinery.com
www.roberthallwinery.com

**Owner:** Robert Hall.

**Location:** 3 miles east of downtown Paso Robles.

**Appellation:** Paso Robles.

**Hours:** 10 A.M.–5 P.M. daily in winter, 10 A.M.–6 P.M. daily in summer.

**Tastings:** $5 for 6 wines; $10 for 6 reserve wines.

**Tours:** Winery and wine caverns with barrel tasting upon request.

**The Wines:** Cabernet Sauvignon, Chardonnay, Grenache Blanc, Merlot, Orange Muscat, Petite Sirah, Sauvignon Blanc, Syrah, Viognier.

**Specialties:** Estate Bordeaux- and Rhône-style blends, port-style wines.

**Winemaker:** Don Brady.

**Annual Production:** 75,000 cases.

**Of Special Note:** Bocce ball court. Garden terrace for picnicking. Locally made food items, books, and wine accessories sold in tasting room.

**Nearby Attractions:** Paso Robles City Park (site of festivals, summer concerts, farmers' market); Estrella Warbird Museum (restored military aircraft, memorabilia).

# SAUCELITO CANYON VINEYARD

**SAUCELITO CANYON VINEYARD**
3080 Biddle Ranch Rd.
San Luis Obispo,
CA 93401
805-543-2111
info@saucelitocanyon.com
www.saucelitocanyon.com

**OWNERS:**
Greenough family.

**LOCATION:** Edna Valley, 7 miles east of Pismo Beach and 6 miles southeast of San Luis Obispo.

**APPELLATION:** Arroyo Grande Valley.

**HOURS:** 10 A.M.–5 P.M. daily.

**TASTINGS:** $8 for 6 wines; $10 for 6 reserve wines.

**TOURS:** None.

**THE WINES:** Cabernet Sauvignon blend, Roussanne/Viognier blend, Sauvignon Blanc, Semillon, Tempranillo, Zinfandel, Zinfandel blends, Zinfandel Late Harvest.

**SPECIALTIES:** Zinfandel, Zinfandel blends.

**WINEMAKER:**
Tom Greenough.

**ANNUAL PRODUCTION:**
4,500 cases.

**OF SPECIAL NOTE:** Estate contains the oldest vineyard in San Luis Obispo County, planted in 1880. Special events include Roll Out the Barrels (third weekend in June) and Harvest Festival (first weekend in November). Patio with picnic tables. Pet friendly. All wines except Sauvignon Blanc and two of the eight Zinfandels are available only in tasting room.

**NEARBY ATTRACTIONS:**
San Luis Obispo County Historical Museum and other historic buildings in downtown San Luis Obispo; Pismo State Beach (swimming, hiking, camping).

In 1880 homesteader Henry Ditmas planted Zinfandel vines on three rugged acres in Saucelito Canyon, tucked in the foothills eight hundred feet above sea level at the eastern terminus of the sixteen-mile Arroyo Grande Valley, just above the fog line. The dry-farmed vines thrived for decades in the balanced climate of reliable sunshine and cool marine breezes. However, the vineyard was abandoned by the 1940s, and dry scrub brush and poison oak eventually shrouded the vines.

Nearly a century later, in 1974, Santa Barbara native Bill Greenough camped out at the remote property he was considering for purchase. Greenough had grown up in Montecito near Mountain Drive, Santa Barbara's legendary bohemian community. His brother, George Greenough, became a famous surfer and surfboard design innovator. But the Mountain Drive group's annual grape stomps and winemaking festivities inspired Greenough to pursue a more land-based career. He drove around with his buddies, winemaking pioneers Michael Benedict and Richard Sanford, searching for land with good grape-growing potential. Sanford and Benedict found their ideal spot in the Santa Rita Hills in 1970. Greenough decided to keep looking, until he finally discovered Rancho Saucelito (Spanish for "little willows"), which Ditmas's granddaughter had put on the market. While camping, he poked around the overgrowth and noticed grape clusters. The 1880 vines were amazingly still alive, convincing Greenough to seal the deal.

Greenough acquired the property on the Fourth of July, 1974. He painstakingly retrained the old vines in the original three-acre plot, and planted an additional five acres in 1976 with Zinfandel and Bordeaux varieties. At first Greenough sold most of his estate grapes to others, but he eventually decided to retain them and become a professional winemaker. He celebrated his first commercial harvest in 1980 and his first bottling in 1982. More than thirty years later, Saucelito Canyon still dry-farms the original self-rooted Zinfandel vineyard and practices sustainable farming throughout the estate. It also remains a small, family-run operation. Bill's wife, Nancy, has helped run the business since the early years. Their three children grew up on the vineyard, and son Tom recently took the helm as winemaker and vineyard manager.

Saucelito Canyon's fascinating story comes to life in the casual, Craftsman-style tasting room, set on ten pastoral acres in the heart of the Edna Valley. Photos of the historic vineyard from as early as 1878 fill the walls, and a small, modest space in front has a tasting bar. On fine-weather days, tasters sit at picnic tables on the patio. Nancy and Bill Greenough often walk through, happy to answer questions about their handcrafted wines and unusual vineyard tale.

# STANGER

The agricultural adventure that gave rise to Stanger vineyards began when Illinois natives Roger and Cheryl Janakus bought a Chicago-area home. The garden harbored a handful of grapevines, which Roger eagerly tended, while remembering happy boyhood summers on his uncle's farm. Seeking respite from the demands of their business—a company that supplies windows to the construction industry—the couple bought a lakeside retreat in southwestern Michigan. They planted a variety of French wine grapes, but, after several discouraging years, decided to head west for a better shot at growing quality fruit.

In 1998 the Janakuses began looking for vineyard property in California. After a two-year search, they purchased 178 acres in the coastal foothills west of Paso Robles. The pair installed water wells, irrigation systems, two miles of road, and 9,000 feet of deer fencing, before planting ten acres to Syrah, Tempranillo, Cabernet Sauvignon, and Pinot Noir. The first fruit was harvested in 2004 and bottled under the Stanger label, a name chosen to honor Roger's maternal ancestor, Daniel Stanger. Stanger, who emigrated from France to the United States in 1833, was among the first Europeans to settle in the Chicago area. The wine is 100 percent estate grown and made at Paso Robles Wine Services, northeast of downtown Paso Robles. After the wine is bottled, the Janakuses age it for two to three years before sending it to market. This generous aging program yields complex vintages that are well developed and accessible upon release.

The Janakuses purchased an additional 165 acres near the tiny town of Creston in 2005 and opened a tasting room on the property three years later. The tasting room is in a farmhouse that sits on a gentle rise. Picnic tables and an outdoor tasting bar offer views of neighboring vineyards. Permanently parked under a tree near the driveway, an orange 1949 Chevrolet flatbed truck holds a load of empty, weathered wine barrels. A converted family room, the 1,600-square-foot tasting room features a brick fireplace and a side door of stained glass and Brazilian mahogany. Placed atop a half-dozen wine barrels, a slab of Red Dragon granite serves as the tasting bar. Original oil paintings depicting Daniel Stanger's Alsatian homeland decorate the cream-colored walls.

Visitors can also sample wine on the west side of Paso Robles, in a tasting room the Janakuses share with Poalillo Vineyards. Located on Vineyard Drive, it is built of reclaimed barn wood and corrugated steel. An umbrella-shaded terrace provides outdoor seating with views of the oak woodland. A natural raconteur, Roger can often be found at one of the two scenic tasting rooms, pouring wine and regaling customers from behind the bar.

**STANGER**

**EASTSIDE**
5525 Hwy. 41 East
Paso Robles, CA 93446
805-238-4777

**WESTSIDE**
7970 Vineyard Dr.
Paso Robles, CA 93446
805-238-0621
roger@stangervineyards.
com
www.stangervineyards.
com

**OWNERS:** Roger and Cheryl Janakus.

**LOCATION:** Eastside: 15 miles east of U.S. 101. Westside: 6 miles north of the intersection of Vineyard Dr. and Hwy. 46 West.

**APPELLATION:** Paso Robles.

**HOURS:** Eastside: 11 A.M.–5 P.M. Friday–Sunday and by appointment. Westside: daily, 11 A.M. until the last taster leaves.

**TASTINGS:** $10 for 4 reserve wines (applicable to purchase).

**TOURS:** None.

**THE WINES:** Cabernet Sauvignon, Cuvée, Pinot Noir, Syrah, Tempranillo.

**SPECIALTIES:** Estate wines and red blends.

**WINEMAKER:** Chris Rougeot.

**ANNUAL PRODUCTION:** 1,200 cases.

**OF SPECIAL NOTE:** Outside seating and picnic area at both locations. Most wines available in tasting rooms only.

**NEARBY ATTRACTIONS:** Town of Creston (country store, Friday night barbecue, September rodeo); Olivas de Oro Olive Company (100-year-old olive trees, olive oil tasting).

# STEPHEN ROSS

**STEPHEN ROSS**
178 Suburban Rd.
San Luis Obispo,
CA 93401
805-594-1318
info@stephenrosswine.com
www.stephenrosswine.com

**OWNERS:** Stephen and
Paula Dooley.

**LOCATION:** 5 minutes
from downtown San Luis
Obispo and the Edna
Valley.

**APPELLATION:** Edna Valley.

**HOURS:** 11 A.M.–5 P.M.
Thursday–Sunday.

**TASTINGS:** $7 for 5 or
6 wines (all reserve).

**TOURS:** Impromptu tours,
self-guided or led by
tasting room staff.

**THE WINES:** Chardonnay,
Petite Sirah, Pinot Noir,
Zinfandel; tiny amounts
of others.

**SPECIALTIES:** Small-lot,
single-vineyard Chardon-
nay and Pinot Noir.

**WINEMAKER:**
Stephen Dooley.

**ANNUAL PRODUCTION:**
4,000 cases.

**OF SPECIAL NOTE:** The
winery hosts special events
in January, June, and
November. Food-and-wine
pairings available on re-
quest. Many wines available
only in the tasting room.

**NEARBY ATTRACTIONS:**
Mission San Luis Obispo
de Tolosa; San Luis Obispo
County Historical Mu-
seum and other historic
buildings in downtown
San Luis Obispo; Pismo
State Beach (swimming,
hiking, camping).

When it comes to making handcrafted wines using classic Burgundian methods and a creative style, few can claim as much experience as Stephen Ross Dooley. His passion for winemaking dates to 1972, when a *Time* magazine article about the emerging U.S. wine industry caught his attention. Then a college freshman in Minnesota, Dooley saw viticulture as a way to combine agriculture and artistry. He eventually earned an enology degree from the University of California, Davis, and worked at legendary Louis Martini in Napa Valley for ten years. He also traveled to Australia and South Africa to work harvests, and became winemaker and general manager at San Luis Obispo. In 1994 label, Stephen Ross (his a custom crush winery in wines at various facilities quickly garnering accolades

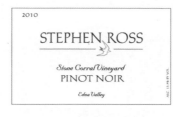

Edna Valley Vineyard near Dooley started his own first and middle names), at Santa Maria. He made his for more than a decade, for excellent Pinot Noir and Chardonnay. The entire time, he looked for a suitable site to establish his own facility.

In 2008 Dooley's quest came to fruition. He and his wife, Paula, discovered a spacious warehouse amid dairy farms, vineyards, and business parks at the southern edge of the city of San Luis Obispo. Dooley set up the state-of-the-art facility for a single purpose: to make exceptional wines. Everything in the tasting room is designed to enable visitors to focus on the wines. The all-white counter on the cherry-finished bar, for example, helps tasters appreciate the color of the wines. There is no gift shop, and only a handful of items are for sale apart from bottles of wines, primarily Pinot Noir and Chardonnay, plus small quantities of other varieties. Dooley sources Pinot Noir grapes from Stone Corral Vineyard in the Edna Valley, planted in 2001, which he owns in partnership with two local wineries. He also obtains small lots from several of Central California's most respected vineyards. Soil samples from present and past sources are displayed on a windowsill, and visitors are invited to touch and sniff them.

A visit to the winery is much like being welcomed into a winemaker's family home. Dooley built a long Shaker-style table with poplar planks and alder end boards, which comfortably seats twelve, in a nook under a stairwell. Photos of Stone Corral Vineyard adorn the walls, and a demonstration garden with thirty Pinot Noir vines graces the entrance. Winery staff members, along with wife Paula, take turns pouring tastes in addition to performing other wine-related tasks. Guided and self-guided tours of the facility are always available. Dooley is often on hand to share details of his passion for crafting wine in his prized facility.

# Tablas Creek Vineyard

Truly a family affair, Tablas Creek Vineyard represents the culmination of two families' dreams to grow and make Rhône-style wines in California. In 1989 the Haas family, East Coast wine importers with fifty years of experience, partnered with the Perrins, proprietors of Châteauneuf du Pape's Château de Beaucastel since 1909, to establish an estate winery with vines sourced from the Perrins' renowned vineyard in France. Robert Haas first met the late Jacques Perrin in 1967 while in Europe scouting for vintages to import to his father's Manhattan wine shop. It took Perrin three years to agree to a deal, but so successful was the arrangement that, after Perrin's death, his sons named Haas their exclusive United States importer. The friendship between the families continued to grow and, twenty years later, led to their decision to start a winery from scratch.

The two families scoured the remote corners of California for a suitable site and purchased 120 acres on the west side of Paso Robles after spotting chalky outcroppings nearby that mimicked the limestone-based soils at Château de Beaucastel. They imported vine cuttings from Rhône varietals growing in the Perrins' vineyard in France, waited three years for them to clear the USDA-mandated quarantine, and finally began propagation in 1993.

Robert's son, Jason, a partner and general manager of Tablas Creek Vineyard, estimates that the nursery propagated 200,000 vines a year until moving off-site in 2004. It sold so many cuttings that Rhône-loving winemakers up and down the state began referring to the winery as "the mother ship." In 1997 the families harvested the first fruit from their organically farmed vineyard and, two years later, released their inaugural wines. Although the master plan did not initially include a tasting room, the partners soon realized that in a region famed for its Bordeaux-style wines, they needed to spread the word about Rhônes.

Opened in 2002 and expanded in 2011, the tasting room sits amid a garden of roses, rosemary, and potted grapevines. Glass doors open onto a sheltered patio. To keep groups small and provide a more personal experience, the interior is divided into three rooms with a half-dozen tasting areas, some featuring views into the barrel room. The conversational buzz on a busy day sounds as if it is coming from a living room full of friends rather than a retail space.

Winemaker Neil Collins ferments the wine using native yeasts, which impart characteristic flavors specific to the site. He carefully blends selected varieties and ages the wine primarily in 1,200-gallon oak casks, just as the winemakers at Château de Beaucastel have done for a century.

**Tablas Creek Vineyard**
9339 Adelaida Rd.
Paso Robles, CA 93446
805-237-1231
info@tablascreek.com
www.tablascreek.com

**Owners:** Haas and Perrin families.

**Location:** 12 miles west of U.S. 101.

**Appellation:** Paso Robles.

**Hours:** 10 a.m.–5 p.m. daily.

**Tastings:** $10 for 7–9 wines (applicable to purchase).

**Tours:** 10:30 a.m. and 2 p.m. daily; appointments necessary, except on festival weekends.

**The Wines:** Counoise, Grenache, Grenache Blanc, Marsanne, Mourvèdre, Picpoul Blanc, Roussanne, Syrah, Tannat, Viognier.

**Specialties:** Esprit de Beaucastel (Mourvèdre, Grenache, Syrah, Counoise blend), Esprit de Beaucastel Blanc (Roussanne, Grenache Blanc, Picpoul Blanc blend).

**Winemaker:** Neil Collins.

**Annual Production:** 18,000 cases.

**Of Special Note:** Wines are exclusively Rhône style. Tasting room sells oil made from on-site olive trees, as well as grapevines.

**Nearby Attraction:** Pasolivo Olive Oil (olive oil tasting, specialty salts, vinegar, and lotion, picnicking).

# TALLEY VINEYARDS

**TALLEY VINEYARDS**
3031 Lopez Dr.
Arroyo Grande, CA 93420
800-489-0446
info@talleyvineyards.com
www.talleyvineyards.com

**OWNERS:** Brian and Johnine Talley.

**LOCATION:** 5 miles east of U.S. 101 and Arroyo Grande on Lopez Dr.; 7.5 miles south of San Luis Obispo via Orcutt Rd.

**APPELLATION:** Arroyo Grande Valley.

**HOURS:** 10:30 A.M.– 4:30 P.M. daily.

**TASTINGS:** $6 for 5 wines; $12–$15 for 5 reserve wines.

**TOURS:** Daily half-hour tour by appointment ($15 with tasting, $10 without). Expanded tours Thursday– Monday by appointment: Estate Tour and Tasting ($35), Special Reserve Tasting in Rincon Room ($25).

**THE WINES:** Cabernet Sauvignon, Chardonnay, Pinot Noir, Riesling, Sauvignon Blanc, Syrah.

**SPECIALTIES:** Estate-grown Chardonnay and Pinot Noir.

**WINEMAKER:** Eric Johnson.

**ANNUAL PRODUCTION:** 25,000 cases.

**OF SPECIAL NOTE:** Gift shop with wine accessories, snacks, and condiments. Three picnic areas. Events include San Luis Obispo Vintners Association celebrations (June and November). Small-lot specialty wines, including Riesling, Sauvignon Blanc, Syrah, and Mano Tinta, available only in tasting room.

**NEARBY ATTRACTIONS:** Arroyo Grande Village (Old West downtown with historic walking tour); Pismo State Beach; Lopez Lake (kayaking, mountain biking, fishing).

Farmers for three generations, the Talley family knows how to tend the fertile Arroyo Grande Valley land to grow a range of delectable produce—including premium wine grapes. Oliver Talley began cultivating specialty vegetables here in 1948. In the 1980s, Don Talley, his wife, Rosemary, and his son, Brian, established Talley Vineyards in the heart of the valley and acquired historic property, once part of a Mexican land grant, with a story-laden 1860s adobe residence. Don Talley recognized the potential for growing high-quality Pinot Noir and Chardonnay on the steep hillsides above the adobe and planted a small test plot with five varieties in 1982. His hunch proved correct, and the family founded Talley Vineyards and expanded the business over the years. El Rincon Adobe served as tasting room for a dozen years.

Today the Talleys continue their farming traditions along with the winemaking business. Talley Farms supplies the region with a range of vegetables and fruits. Talley Vineyards, with Brian and his wife, Johnine, at the helm, grows grapes on 190 acres of estate vineyards in the Arroyo Grande and Edna valleys, named Rincon, Rosemary's, Monte Sereno, Las Ventanas, Oliver's, and Stone Corral. Winemaker Eric Johnson, who earned a degree in wine and viticulture studies from California Polytechnic University San Luis Obispo, applies a gentle hand to reflect the *terroir* while crafting vintages in the 8,000-square-foot gravity-flow facility on the Rincon Vineyard property. Johnson's bottlings appear under two different labels. Talley Vineyards wines focus on stellar Chardonnay and Pinot Noir produced entirely from estate vineyards. Wines bearing the label Bishop's Peak reflect the distinct characteristics of various vineyard regions in San Luis Obispo County. The winery also makes Mano Tinta wines, whose proceeds support an endowment benefiting county farmworkers.

Windows in the spacious, Tuscan-style hospitality center, built in 2002, open to spectacular views of Arroyo Grande Valley and Rincon Vineyard. Before and after tasting wines, visitors can browse the exhibits of local art and relax outdoors amid the lush landscaping, which includes a picnic area next to an expansive courtyard. Additional picnic areas near the winery and historic adobe overlook farm fields and Rincon Vineyard. Daily tours take visitors through Rincon Vineyard, the winery, and the barrel room; an expanded tour features a reserve and library tasting. For a full-scale experience, sign up for the longer estate tour, which includes a barrel tasting and a fascinating visit to historic El Rincon Adobe, whose image appears on every Talley Vineyards label.

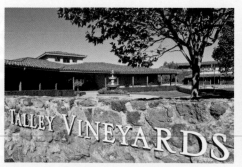

# THACHER WINERY

One hundred sixty apple trees — ten each of sixteen varieties suitable for making hard cider — flank the driveway to Thacher Winery. The road ends at a farmlike compound anchored by a 7,000-square-foot gray barn with a distinctively rounded roof. The ninety-year-old landmark bears the initials KR, taken from a livestock brand reflecting the property's historic name, Kentucky Ranch. Opposite the barn, owners Michelle and Sherman Thacher built a 4,600-square-foot, solar-powered winery with slot windows and arched pine doors. On the porch stand a red horse-drawn carriage that belonged to Sherman's maternal great-great-grandmother and a ranch wagon once used in her family's historic Ventura County orchards.

A fifth-generation Californian, Sherman was raised in Ojai, where his paternal great-grandfather tended a citrus

orchard and, in 1887, founded a renowned boarding school. Following in the family's footsteps, Sherman farms a small Zinfandel and Petite Sirah vineyard. He buys additional fruit to supplement his wine production, preferring Paso Robles–area grapes because of their diverse flavor profiles.

Shortly after graduating from U.C. Davis in 1991, Sherman joined a beer-making friend at a Bay Area brewery, where he would spend sixteen years. He learned on the job and in four years became brewmaster. For fun, he made small batches of wine on the side. Sherman met Michelle at the brewery, and when she moved to Santa Barbara to attend college, the couple routinely rendezvoused in Paso Robles. They spent countless weekends touring the region and dreaming of owning a winery. Six years after marrying in 1998, they purchased the fifty-two-acre Kentucky Ranch.

In 2008 the Thachers completed the winery and a tasting room skirted by an inviting patio with a water fountain. A wraparound porch holds one-of-a-kind tables and chairs that were crafted from old wine barrels by Sherman's father. Perched atop the tasting room, a grasshopper-shaped weathervane pays tribute to the medieval grasshoppers emblazoned on the Thacher family crest and wine labels. The five-hundred-square-foot tasting room resembles a small farmhouse. Inside, rotating exhibits of original paintings adorn the walls, and even the copper bar top, with its constellation of colors left by unintentional splashes of wine, lends an artistic touch. Behind the bar, a bottle of Viognier chills in a gourd that was fashioned for the purpose. Wood-framed windows afford long views of gently rolling hills, sycamore-studded pastures that are home to a flock of family goats, and tin-roofed stables.

THACHER WINERY
8355 Vineyard Dr.
Paso Robles, CA 93446
805-237-0087
info@thacherwinery.com
www.thacherwinery.com

OWNERS: Sherman and Michelle Thacher.

LOCATION: 7 miles northwest of the intersection of Hwy. 46 West and Vineyard Dr.

APPELLATIONS: Monterey, Paso Robles.

HOURS: 11 A.M.–5 P.M. Thursday–Monday.

TASTINGS: $10 for 6–8 wines (applicable to purchase of 2 or more bottles).

TOURS: By appointment.

THE WINES: Grenache, Grenache Blanc, Mourvèdre, Syrah, Viognier, Zinfandel.

SPECIALTIES: Rhône-style blends, Zinfandel.

WINEMAKER: Sherman Thacher.

ANNUAL PRODUCTION: 1,800 cases.

OF SPECIAL NOTE: Patio and picnic tables.

NEARBY ATTRACTIONS: Farmstead 46 (deli, organic gardens); Pasolivo Olive Oil (olive oil tasting, specialty vinegars, salts, and lotions, picnicking).

# TOBIN JAMES CELLARS

**TOBIN JAMES CELLARS**
8950 Union Rd.
Paso Robles, CA 93446
805-239-2204
info@tobinjames.com
www.tobinjames.com

**OWNERS:** Tobin James, Lance and Claire Silver.

**LOCATION:** 9 miles east of downtown Paso Robles.

**APPELLATION:** Paso Robles.

**HOURS:** 10 A.M.–6 P.M. daily.

**TASTINGS:** Complimentary.

**TOURS:** None.

**THE WINES:** Barbera, Cabernet Franc, Cabernet Sauvignon, Chardonnay, Lagrein, Malbec, Merlot, Petit Verdot, Sangiovese, Sauvignon Blanc, sparkling wines, Syrah, Tempranillo, Zinfandel, dessert wines.

**SPECIALTIES:** Chateau Le Cacheflo (red blend), Estate Private Stash (Bordeaux blend), 5 (Bordeaux blend), Zinfandel.

**WINEMAKERS:** Tobin James, Lance Silver, Claire Silver, Jeff Poe.

**ANNUAL PRODUCTION:** 50,000 cases.

**OF SPECIAL NOTE:** Outdoor patio for picnicking. Free video games. Many limited-production wines available only in the tasting room.

**NEARBY ATTRACTIONS:** Barney Schwartz Park (lake, picnic areas); Estrella Warbird Museum (restored military aircraft, memorabilia).

On the eastern edge of the Paso Robles appellation stands a wine country outpost steeped in the worthy tradition of western hospitality. Built on the site of a nineteenth-century stagecoach stop, Tobin James Cellars welcomes guests into a tasting room reminiscent of a Gold Rush–era saloon, complete with a grand antique mahogany bar, opulent red wallpaper, and lively music. Ceiling fans stir the air, while Victorian-style light fixtures illuminate a visual carnival of cowboy hats, large-format bottled wines, brass rails, lace curtains, and state fair ribbons. Origami dollar bills festoon an old-fashioned cash register, and two other tasting bars, built of matching mahogany, tell a tale of revelry.

Tobin James and his business partners, Lance and Claire Silver, want visitors to feel right at home, so they offer wine-friendly appetizers, wine samples, and family-friendly video games free of charge. In Claire Silver's view, the secret to the winery's overwhelming success lies in the owners' and staff's desire to give customers more than they expect.

Born in San Francisco, Tobin James was raised in Indiana, where his family's vineyard and wine-making activities caught his fancy at an early age. While working in his brother's Ohio wine shop, he met and received an offer to work crush from pioneering Paso Robles vintner Gary Eberle and, in 1980, happily headed west. James worked with Eberle for more than ten years, served as Peachy Canyon Winery's founding winemaker, and in 1994 built his own facility. Two years later, he formed a dynamic partnership with Lance and Claire Silver and in 2003 hired winemaker Jeff Poe to help handle the growing production at a winery that claims to observe only one rule: "have fun."

The winery's estate vineyard is twenty acres, and the winery sources the best red wine grapes from all over the appellation, as well as whites from cooler regions in Arroyo Grande and Monterey County. The winemakers blend Zinfandel from forty different vineyards, including one that is eighty-five years old, and view the variety as a mighty spice rack from which to blend and create award-winning wines of remarkable depth and complexity.

After tasting, visitors who would like to enjoy some wine over a picnic lunch can head to the outdoor patio, a grotto of stone, brick, and glistening tile that easily qualifies as architectural art. From here, they can see the logo on the label mirrored in the distance as the glimmering sun sets over the wild, western hills of Paso Robles.

# TREANA AND HOPE FAMILY WINES

ioneers of the Paso Robles wine industry, Chuck and Marlyn Hope are second-generation farmers who moved to the Central Coast in 1978. Seeking new opportunities, they left Bakersfield to plant apple trees along the Salinas River. They also planted a vineyard that included Cabernet Sauvignon. As apple sales lagged, the couple devoted their efforts to growing quality wine grapes. The vineyard was a family affair, and even their eight-year-old son Austin helped by hoeing weeds from between the vines.

By the late 1980s the Hopes were selling Cabernet Sauvignon to the renowned Caymus Vineyards in Napa Valley. They developed a close relationship with the winery's owner, Chuck Wagner, and were among the first to tap Paso Robles' potential for producing stellar red wines. The Hopes launched their debut label, Hope Family Farms, in the early 1990s, just as Chuck Hope helped organize the Paso Robles Vintners and Growers Association.

In 1994, following the family's lead, Austin took a job at Caymus Vineyards. With Wagner as a mentor, he received an in-depth wine industry education. In 1995 Austin traveled to France to learn Rhône-style winemaking. Later that year he graduated from Cal Poly, San Luis Obispo, with a degree in fruit science and became assistant winemaker at Hope Family Farms. In 1996 the family founded Treana Winery, a label devoted to their signature Rhône-influenced blends. Two years later, Austin was making the flagship Treana Red. In 2009 the forty-acre Hope Family Vineyard earned Sustainability in Practice certification through a program that promotes sustainable farming. That same year the family created Hope Family Wines, under which they currently make five distinct labels sold in fifty states and ten countries. To support production, the Hopes buy additional fruit from fifty local vineyards.

At the winery, Grenache vines climb wooden stakes, suggesting a vineyard in the Rhône region. Valley oaks shade the wildlife corridor that skirts the sixty-two-acre property, which includes the family's estate vineyard. Three cedar-clad buildings served as a winery and two barrel rooms until 2009, when the Hopes converted one of the barrel rooms into an elegant tasting cellar. Inside, visitors walk between wine-filled oak barrels. Dividing the 3,000-square-foot room are two curved structures forming a grand entryway into the tasting area. Built from quarter-split white oak, they resemble wine casks wrapped with steel hoops. The barrel theme repeats at the tasting counter, where the front of the zinc-topped bar is made of white oak planks fitted with steel bands. In the white wall behind the bar, a half-dozen windows of varying sizes frame vibrant oak tree and vineyard views.

---

**TREANA AND HOPE FAMILY WINES**
1585 Live Oak Rd.
Paso Robles, CA 93446
805-238-4112
info@hfwines.com
www.hopefamilywines.com

**OWNERS:** Hope family.

**LOCATION:** 1 mile west of U.S. 101, just off Hwy. 46 West.

**APPELLATION:** Paso Robles.

**HOURS:** 10 A.M.–4 P.M. Friday and Saturday, and by appointment.

**TASTINGS:** Complimentary for 5 wines; $10 for 10 wines.

**TOURS:** By appointment.

**THE WINES:** Cabernet Sauvignon, Chardonnay, Grenache, Marsanne, Merlot, Mourvèdre, Roussanne, Syrah, Viognier, Zinfandel.

**SPECIALTIES:** Treana Red (Cabernet Sauvignon, Syrah blend); Treana White (Viognier, Marsanne blend).

**WINEMAKERS:** Austin Hope, Jason Diefenderfer.

**ANNUAL PRODUCTION:** 250,000 cases.

**OF SPECIAL NOTE:** The winery also bottles wine under the Austin Hope, Candor, Troublemaker, and Liberty School labels, which are available for tasting in the tasting cellar. Annual bacon-and-wine pairing event in May.

**NEARBY ATTRACTION:** Paso Robles City Park (site of festivals, summer concerts, farmers' market).

# VINA ROBLES

**VINA ROBLES**
3700 Mill Rd.
Paso Robles, CA 93446
805-227-4812
info@vinarobles.com
www.vinarobles.com

**OWNER:** Hans Nef.

**LOCATION:** 3 miles east of
U.S. 101, off Hwy. 46 East.

**APPELLATION:** Paso Robles.

**HOURS:** 10 A.M.–5 P.M.
daily in winter, 10 A.M.–
6 P.M. daily in summer.

**TASTINGS:** $7 for 5
estate wines; $10 for
reserve tasting, including
Cuvée Collection.

**TOURS:** None.

**THE WINES:** Cabernet
Sauvignon, Petit Verdot,
Petite Sirah, Sauvignon
Blanc, Syrah.

**SPECIALTIES:** Estate blends
such as Red[4] and White[4],
Signature, Syrée, and
Suendero.

**WINEMAKER:**
Kevin Willenborg.

**ANNUAL PRODUCTION:**
30,000 cases.

**OF SPECIAL NOTE:** Food-
and-wine pairings offered
daily. Gift shop featuring
gourmet foods and cook-
books. Deli section with
artisan cheeses. Terrace,
patio, and lawn areas for
picnicking. Art exhibit on
display. Ongoing free live
music, scheduled biweekly.

**NEARBY ATTRACTIONS:**
Barney Schwartz Park
(lake, picnic areas); Estrella
Warbird Museum (restored
military aircraft, memo-
rabilia).

A red-roofed showplace that draws visitors from around the world, the Vina Robles hospitality center opened in 2007, ten years after its owner, Swiss entrepreneur Hans Nef, planted his four estate vineyards on the east side of Paso Robles. Nef built the winery and center with a variety of events in mind—from barbecues and concerts to banquets and conferences—and created a wonderfully functional complex of terraces, courtyards, and indoor spaces. Pillars and thick walls composed of carefully fitted stones lend dramatic mass to the structures and reflect a style inspired by California's climate and Franciscan missions. A large arbor supported by stone columns joins two heri-  tage oaks in shading the entryway, as soft music drifts about the courtyard and blends with the pleasing sound of water in nearby fountains.

Inside, visitors can wander through the gift shop stocked with locally produced items, kitchenware, crystal glasses, and gourmet goodies before heading into the impressive tasting area. Just past the exposed stone walls of the foyer, a massive fireplace promises winter warmth, large artworks inspired by the vineyard hang below a row of lofty windows, and a sheer sense of space prevails. In front of a huge, arched window that looks over the demonstration vineyard, stacked glassware glints from behind the triangular concrete bar. Here, wine aficionados may enjoy complimentary samples of the winemaker's choice of the month or pay a nominal fee to taste a selection of estate wines and sip the Cuvée Collection of signature blends.

Marc Laderriere, vice president of sales, notes that, because of the winery's Swiss heritage, its principals embrace a "European approach" that favors food-friendly wines with modest alcohol content and a bright finish. To promote the enjoyment of wine with food, the winery offers a number of wine-and-food pairings. They include a creative pairing of five artisan cheeses and special release wines, the Petite Sirah and Chocolate Experience featuring locally made truffles, and the Gourmet Lunch Tasting, which begins with a sampling of wines, followed by a sumptuous meal. A Day at Vina Robles is an event tailored for each group and might start with a vineyard tour, followed by lunch and a tasting of current releases. Participants practice what they've learned about winemaking by creating their own unique blends and then tuck into a lavish barbecue dinner at the winery.

In addition to wine tasting, the hospitality center hosts a variety of innovative events, including a series showcasing the region's finest food and music, and rotating art exhibits in the gallery. Every other Saturday, visitors can taste Vina Robles wines to the accompaniment of live music.

# WILD HORSE WINERY

One of the oldest producers in the region, Wild Horse Winery completed its first crush in 1983, the year that Paso Robles became an official appellation. Named for the wild mustangs that once roamed the neighboring hills, it remains a local favorite, renowned for its eclectic portfolio of wines, prolific organic vegetable garden, and Floyd, the resident llama.

Wild Horse chose the east side of Paso Robles for its vineyard because of the area's low-vigor soils, believing their lean constitution would force the sustainably farmed vineyard to produce grapes with highly concentrated flavors. As an ambitious experiment, forty-five acres were planted with thirty-three varietals, some of them considered unusual even by today's standards. Among the blocks of Chardonnay and Cabernet Sauvignon were heirlooms like Verdelho, Blaufränkisch, and Malvasia Bianca, from which the winery still produces tasting-room-exclusive vintages. Vineyard workers continue to employ the sustainable methods used early on by the winery. They brew compost tea to feed the vines, use a state-of-the-art water recycling system, and compost the pomace left behind by the grape presses. Sheep are used for weed control and are protected from coyotes by Floyd.

The winery and tasting room lie beyond two ranch-style gates and at the end of a long road bordered by vineyards. Leading to the tasting room on the ground floor of a two-story complex is a wooden pergola that bisects a lawn and patio set with tables and chairs. Flower beds edge the grass, and half barrels planted with New Zealand flax and trailing succulents line the shaded path to the tasting room door. An equine theme informs the decor of the intimate room, where tan plantation shutters filter sunlight and Saltillo floor tiles enhance the western flavor. A framed photo of three wild mustangs mirrors the winery's logo horse as it gallops across hats, T-shirts, and wine bottles. Display tables and shelves, some crafted from old wine barrels, offer a diverse assortment of books, wine accessories, jams, nut brittle, and local olive oil. At the white oak tasting bar, visitors can sample selections from wine lists aptly titled Unbridled, the Four Horsemen, and Cheval Sauvage.

Today, the estate vineyard provides about 4 percent of the fruit needed to fuel the facility's extensive varietal program, so every fall winemakers Clay Brock and Chrissy Wittmann select from grapes grown in more than forty Central Coast vineyards, some of which have been supplying the winery since its inception.

**WILD HORSE WINERY**
1437 Wild Horse Winery Ct.
Templeton, CA 93465
805-788-6300
leslie.churchill@
iconestateswine.com
www.wildhorsewinery.com

**LOCATION:** 10 miles south of Paso Robles.

**APPELLATION:** Paso Robles.

**HOURS:** 11 A.M.–5 P.M. daily.

**TASTINGS:** $5 for 5 wines; $10 with wineglass.

**TOURS:** None.

**THE WINES:** Blaufränkisch, Cabernet Sauvignon, Chardonnay, Malvasia Bianca, Merlot, Pinot Noir, Verdelho, Viognier.

**SPECIALTIES:** Cheval Sauvage (Pinot Noir), Pinot Noir.

**WINEMAKERS:** Clay Brock, Chrissy Wittmann.

**ANNUAL PRODUCTION:** 200,000 cases.

**OF SPECIAL NOTE:** Patio for picnicking. Gift shop featuring local olive oil, wine accessories, and other items. Free organic produce in season. Heirloom and Unbridled wines available only in tasting room.

**NEARBY ATTRACTIONS:** Barney Schwartz Park (lake, picnic areas); Estrella Warbird Museum (restored military aircraft, memorabilia).

# CENTRAL COAST WINE VARIETALS

The wineries in this book currently produce the following wines, as well as many unique, proprietary blends. Before you visit a tasting room to sample or purchase a particular wine variety, contact the winery to make sure it is available.

**ALBARIÑO**
Qupé

**BARBERA**
Bianchi Winery & Tasting Room
Eberle Winery
Tobin James Cellars

**BLAUFRÄNKISCH**
Wild Horse Winery

**CABERNET FRANC**
Bianchi Winery & Tasting Room
Buttonwood Farm Winery & Vineyard
Carr Vineyards & Winery
foxen 7200
HammerSky Vineyards
Hearthstone Vineyard & Winery
Hitching Post Wines
Mondo Cellars
Niner Wine Estates
Peachy Canyon Winery
Tobin James Cellars

**CABERNET SAUVIGNON**
Barrel 27 Wine Company
Bianchi Winery & Tasting Room
Buttonwood Farm Winery & Vineyard
Calcareous Vineyard
Cass Winery
Chateau Margene
Clayhouse Wines
Costa de Oro Winery
Eberle Winery
foxen 7200
Gainey Vineyard
Halter Ranch Vineyard
HammerSky Vineyards
Hearthstone Vineyard & Winery
J. Lohr Vineyards & Wines
Justin Vineyards & Winery
Lincourt Winery
Mondo Cellars
Niner Wine Estates
Opolo Vineyards
Peachy Canyon Winery
Penman Springs Vineyard
Pomar Junction Vineyard & Winery
Robert Hall Winery
Stanger
Talley Vineyards
Tobin James Cellars
Treana and Hope Family Wines
Vina Robles
Wild Horse Winery

**CHARDONNAY**
Alma Rosa Winery & Vineyards
Bianchi Winery & Tasting Room
Calcareous Vineyard
Cambria Estate Winery
Chamisal Vineyards
Costa de Oro Winery
D'Alfonso-Curran Wines
Eberle Winery
Foley Estates Vineyard & Winery
Foxen
Gainey Vineyard
J. Lohr Vineyards & Wines
Justin Vineyards & Winery
Laetitia Vineyard & Winery
Lafond Winery & Vineyards
Lincourt Winery
Loring Wine Company
Opolo Vineyards
Pomar Junction Vineyard & Winery
Presqu'ile Winery
Qupé
Robert Hall Winery
Stephen Ross
Talley Vineyards
Tobin James Cellars
Treana and Hope Family Wines
Wild Horse Winery
Zaca Mesa Winery & Vineyards

**CHENIN BLANC**
Foxen

**CINSAULT**
Zaca Mesa Winery & Vineyards

**COUNOISE**
Tablas Creek Vineyard

**DESSERT WINE**
Buttonwood Farm Winery & Vineyard
Tobin James Cellars

**GEWÜRZTRAMINER**
Tercero Wines

**GRENACHE**
Andrew Murray Vineyards
Blair Fox Cellars
Buttonwood Farm Winery & Vineyard
Carr Vineyards & Winery
Cass Winery
Chamisal Vineyards
Chateau Margene
D'Alfonso-Curran Wines
Foxen
Hearthstone Vineyard & Winery
J. Lohr Vineyards & Wines
Lafond Winery & Vineyards

Mondo Cellars
Opolo Vineyards
Qupé
Tablas Creek Vineyard
Tercero Wines
Thacher Winery
Treana and Hope Family Wines
Zaca Mesa Winery & Vineyards

**GRENACHE BLANC**
Andrew Murray Vineyards
Barrel 27 Wine Company
Buttonwood Farm Winery & Vineyard
Chateau Margene
Clayhouse Wines
D'Alfonso-Curran Wines
Mondo Cellars
Niner Wine Estates
Robert Hall Winery
Tablas Creek Vineyard
Tercero Wines
Thacher Winery

**GRENACHE NOIR**
Barrel 27 Wine Company

**GRENACHE ROSÉ**
D'Alfonso-Curran Wines
Halter Ranch Vineyard

**LAGREIN**
Tobin James Cellars

**MALBEC**
Buttonwood Farm Winery & Vineyard
Clayhouse Wines
Niner Wine Estates
Opolo Vineyards
Tobin James Cellars

**MALVASIA BIANCA**
Wild Horse Winery

**MARSANNE**
Buttonwood Farm Winery & Vineyard
Cass Winery
Mondo Cellars
Qupé
Tablas Creek Vineyard
Treana and Hope Family Wines

**MERITAGE**
Calcareous Vineyard
Penman Springs Vineyard

**MERLOT**
Bianchi Winery & Tasting Room
Buttonwood Farm Winery & Vineyard

Carhartt Vineyard
Costa de Oro Winery
D'Alfonso-Curran Wines
foxen 7200
Gainey Vineyard
HammerSky Vineyards
Hitching Post Wines
J. Lohr Vineyards & Wines
Lincourt Winery
Mondo Cellars
Niner Wine Estates
Opolo Vineyards
Peachy Canyon Winery
Penman Springs Vineyard
Pomar Junction Vineyard & Winery
Robert Hall Winery
Tobin James Cellars
Treana and Hope Family Wines
Wild Horse Winery

**MOSCATO**
Barrel 27 Wine Company
Bianchi Winery & Tasting Room

**MOURVÈDRE**
Andrew Murray Vineyards
Barrel 27 Wine Company
Cass Winery
Chateau Margene
Foxen
Hearthstone Vineyard & Winery
J. Lohr Vineyards & Wines
Mondo Cellars
Opolo Vineyards
Tablas Creek Vineyard
Tercero Wines
Thacher Winery
Treana and Hope Family Wines
Zaca Mesa Winery & Vineyards

**MUSCAT BLANC**
Penman Springs Vineyard

**MUSCAT CANELLI**
Eberle Winery
Opolo Vineyards

**NEBBIOLO**
D'Alfonso-Curran Wines

**ORANGE MUSCAT**
Robert Hall Winery

**PETIT VERDOT**
Calcareous Vineyard
HammerSky Vineyards
Opolo Vineyards
Penman Springs Vineyard
Tobin James Cellars
Vina Robles

## PETITE SIRAH
Bianchi Winery & Tasting Room
Blair Fox Cellars
Cass Winery
Chateau Margene
Clayhouse Wines
Hearthstone Vineyard & Winery
J. Lohr Vineyards & Wines
Mondo Cellars
Niner Wine Estates
Opolo Vineyards
Peachy Canyon Winery
Penman Springs Vineyard
Robert Hall Winery
Stephen Ross
Tercero Wines
Vina Robles

## PICPOUL BLANC
Tablas Creek Vineyard

## PINOT BLANC
Alma Rosa Winery & Vineyards
Lincourt Winery

## PINOT GRIGIO
Bianchi Winery & Tasting Room
Costa de Oro Winery
D'Alfonso-Curran Wines
Lincourt Winery
Opolo Vineyards

## PINOT GRIS
Alma Rosa Winery & Vineyards
Cambria Estate Winery
Carr Vineyards & Winery
Chamisal Vineyards

## PINOT NOIR
Alma Rosa Winery & Vineyards
Bianchi Winery & Tasting Room
Calcareous Vineyard
Cambria Estate Winery
Carr Vineyards & Winery
Chamisal Vineyards
Chateau Margene
Costa de Oro Winery
D'Alfonso-Curran Wines
Foley Estates Vineyard & Winery
Foxen
Gainey Vineyard
Hearthstone Vineyard & Winery
Hitching Post Wines
J. Lohr Vineyards & Wines
Laetitia Vineyard & Winery
Lafond Winery & Vineyards
Lincourt Winery
Loring Wine Company
Opolo Vineyards
Pomar Junction Vineyard &
    Winery
Presqu'ile Winery
Stanger
Stephen Ross
Talley Vineyards
Wild Horse Winery

## PORT AND OTHER FORTIFIED WINES
Penman Springs Vineyard

## REFOSCO
Bianchi Winery & Tasting Room

## RIESLING
Gainey Vineyard
J. Lohr Vineyards & Wines
Lafond Winery & Vineyards
Talley Vineyards

## ROSÉ
Buttonwood Farm Winery &
    Vineyard
Carhartt Vineyard
Foley Estates Vineyard & Winery
Hitching Post Wines
Presqu'ile Winery
Zaca Mesa Winery & Vineyards

## ROUSSANNE
Andrew Murray Vineyards
Barrel 27 Wine Company
Calcareous Vineyard
Cass Winery
Hearthstone Vineyard & Winery
Mondo Cellars
Opolo Vineyards
Qupé
Tablas Creek Vineyard
Treana and Hope Family Wines
Zaca Mesa Winery & Vineyards

## SANGIOVESE
Bianchi Winery & Tasting Room
Carhartt Vineyard
Carr Vineyards & Winery
D'Alfonso-Curran Wines
Eberle Winery
foxen 7200
Hearthstone Vineyard & Winery
Niner Wine Estates
Opolo Vineyards
Tobin James Cellars

## SAUVIGNON BLANC
Bianchi Winery & Tasting Room
Buttonwood Farm Winery &
    Vineyard
Carhartt Vineyard
Clayhouse Wines
Costa de Oro Winery
foxen 7200
Gainey Vineyard
Halter Ranch Vineyard
J. Lohr Vineyards & Wines
Justin Vineyards & Winery
Lincourt Winery
Niner Wine Estates
Presqu'ile Winery
Robert Hall Winery
Saucelito Canyon Vineyard
Talley Vineyards
Tobin James Cellars
Vina Robles

## SÉMILLON
Saucelito Canyon Vineyard

## SPARKLING WINE
Laetitia Vineyard & Winery
Tobin James Cellars

## SYRAH
Andrew Murray Vineyards
Barrel 27 Wine Company
Bianchi Winery & Tasting Room
Blair Fox Cellars
Buttonwood Farm Winery &
    Vineyard
Calcareous Vineyard
Cambria Estate Winery
Carhartt Vineyard
Carr Vineyards & Winery
Cass Winery
Chamisal Vineyards
Clayhouse Wines
Costa de Oro Winery
D'Alfonso-Curran Wines
Eberle Winery
Foley Estates Vineyard & Winery
Foxen
Gainey Vineyard
Halter Ranch Vineyard
Hearthstone Vineyard & Winery
Hitching Post Wines
J. Lohr Vineyards & Wines
Justin Vineyards & Winery
Laetitia Vineyard & Winery
Lafond Winery & Vineyards
Lincourt Winery
Mondo Cellars
Niner Wine Estates
Opolo Vineyards
Penman Springs Vineyard
Pomar Junction Vineyard &
    Winery
Presqu'ile Winery
Qupé
Robert Hall Winery
Stanger
Tablas Creek Vineyard
Talley Vineyards
Tercero Wines
Thacher Winery
Tobin James Cellars
Treana and Hope Family Wines
Vina Robles
Zaca Mesa Winery & Vineyards

## TANNAT
Clayhouse Wines
Tablas Creek Vineyard

## TEMPRANILLO
Barrel 27 Wine Company
Clayhouse Wines
Costa de Oro Winery
D'Alfonso-Curran Wines
Hearthstone Vineyard & Winery
Justin Vineyards & Winery
Opolo Vineyards
Qupé
Saucelito Canyon Vineyard
Stanger
Tobin James Cellars

## VALDIGUIÉ
J. Lohr Vineyards & Wines

## VERDELHO
Wild Horse Winery

## VERMENTINO
Blair Fox Cellars

## VIOGNIER
Andrew Murray Vineyards
Barrel 27 Wine Company
Blair Fox Cellars
Calcareous Vineyard
Cambria Estate Winery
Cass Winery
Clayhouse Wines
Eberle Winery
Halter Ranch Vineyard
Hearthstone Vineyard & Winery
J. Lohr Vineyards & Wines
Justin Vineyards & Winery
Opolo Vineyards
Peachy Canyon Winery
Pomar Junction Vineyard &
    Winery
Qupé
Robert Hall Winery
Tablas Creek Vineyard
Tercero Wines
Thacher Winery
Treana and Hope Family Wines
Wild Horse Winery
Zaca Mesa Winery & Vineyards

## ZINFANDEL
Barrel 27 Wine Company
Bianchi Winery & Tasting Room
Calcareous Vineyard
Carhartt Vineyard
Clayhouse Wines
Eberle Winery
HammerSky Vineyards
Hearthstone Vineyard & Winery
J. Lohr Vineyards & Wines
Mondo Cellars
Opolo Vineyards
Peachy Canyon Winery
Pomar Junction Vineyard &
    Winery
Saucelito Canyon Vineyard
Stephen Ross
Thacher Winery
Tobin James Cellars
Treana and Hope Family Wines

Wine House Press
127 East Napa Street, Suite E
Sonoma, CA 95476
707-996-1741

Editor and publisher: Tom Silberkleit
Original design: Jennifer Barry Design
Production: Poulson Gluck Design
Copyeditor: Judith Dunham
Cartographer: Ben Pease
Artistic development: Lisa Silberkleit
Proofreader: Linda Bouchard

All photographs by Robert Holmes, except the following:
page 17, Deborah Cash; page 30, bottom left: courtesy Andrew Murray Vineyards; page 33, bottom left, courtesy Winescapes
Photography; pages 36 and 37, courtesy Cambria Estate Winery; page 45, courtesy D'Alfonso-Curran Wines; page 92, bottom left,
courtesy HammerSky Vineyards; page 95, bottom left, courtesy Hearthstone Vineyard & Winery; pages 122 and 123, bottom right,
courtesy Tablas Creek Vineyard; page 127, bottom right, courtesy Thacher Winery.

Front cover photograph: Chamisal Vineyards, San Luis Obispo
Back cover photographs: top left: Maloy O'Neill Vineyards; top right: Niner Wine Estates;
bottom left: Zaca Mesa Winery & Vineyards; bottom right: Stanger

"What Is an Appellation?," "The Making of Wine," "The Art of Barrel Making," "Modern Stoppers," "The Food and Wine Connection,"
"Reading a Wine Label," and "The Etiquette of Wine Tasting": K. Reka Badger, Cheryl Crabtree, and Marty Olmstead

Printed and bound in Singapore through Imago Sales (USA) Inc.
ISBN-13: 978-0-9724993-7-8

Second Edition

Distributed by Publishers Group West, 1700 4th Street, Berkeley, CA 94710, www.pgw.com

*Customized Editions*
Wine House Press will print custom editions of this volume for bulk purchase at your request. Personalized covers and
foil-stamped corporate logo imprints can be created in large quantities for special promotions or events, or as premiums.
For more information, contact Custom Imprints, Wine House Press, 127 E. Napa Street, Suite E, Sonoma, CA 95476; 707-996-1741.

*Join the Facebook Fan Page: www.facebook.com/CaliforniaFineWineries*
*Follow us on Twitter: twitter.com/cafinewineries*
*Scan to visit our website: www.CaliforniaFineWineries.com*

# ACKNOWLEDGMENTS

Creativity, perseverance, integrity, and commitment are fundamental qualities
for guaranteeing the success of a project. The artistic and editorial teams who worked on
this edition possess these qualities in large measures. My heartfelt thanks go to K. Reka Badger
and Cheryl Crabtree, writers; Robert Holmes, photographer; Judith Dunham, copyeditor;
Linda Bouchard, proofreader; Poulson Gluck Design, production; and Ben Pease, cartographer.

In addition, I am grateful for the invaluable counsel and encouragement of Danny Biederman;
Fran Clow; Jim Fiolek; Christopher Taranto; my esteemed parents—Estelle Silberkleit and William
Silberkleit; and the scores of readers and winery enthusiasts who have contacted me
over the past decade to say how much they enjoy this book series.

I also extend my deepest appreciation to Victor Popp and the staff of La Quinta Inn and Suites
of Paso Robles, California, as well as Bill Gesler and Camden Wirick of the Santa Ynez Valley Marriott,
for their superb hospitality and enthusiastic support of this project. Special thanks also go to
Maurice Boyd of Fess Parker's Santa Barbara County Wine Center
for lending critical logistic assistance.

And finally, for her love and creative input, as well as for enduring work-filled weekends
and midnight deadlines, my gratitude and affection go to Lisa Silberkleit.

— Tom Silberkleit

OTHER BOOKS BY WINE HOUSE PRESS

**The California Directory of Fine Wineries — Northern Region**
*Napa • Sonoma • Mendocino*